Anchors
of Hope

Anchors of Hope

Words of Life for the Soul

Volume One

Hal M. Helms

PARACLETE PRESS
Brewster, Massachusetts

Library of Congress Cataloging-in-Publication Data

Helms, Hal McElwaine.
Anchors of Hope/Hal M. Helms.
p.cm.
Contents: v. 1. Words of life for the soul.
ISBN 1-55725-172-X
1. Aged—Prayer-books and devotions—English.
2. Aging—Religious aspects—Christianity—
    Meditations. 3. Devotional calendars.
I.Title.
BV4580.H33   1996
242'.65—dc20   96-34156
                                        CIP

10 9 8 7 6 5 4 3 2 1

© 1996 by Paraclete Press
ISBN #: 1-55725-172-X

Published by Paraclete Press,
Brewster, Massachusetts
Printed in the United States of America.

Cover photo credit:
photo # C000-15321-153; Comstock Inc.

Table of Contents

Foreword

We do not know how much hope can mean to us until we are deprived of some of the many things we have taken for granted. It may be health. It may be the restrictions that age brings on and the loss of freedom we had always known. It may be other circumstances that we find difficult to face.

The "living hope" which Almighty God gives to His children is the overarching theme of this book. It is sent forth to those who are struggling with life's difficulties. It is intended to sound a note of encouragement day by day, so that instead of majoring on the difficulties, we can major on the fact that God is, that He has created us, sustained us and that His promises are for *today*. One of the most popular hymns today is "Amazing Grace." The second stanza says, "Through many dangers, toils and snares, I have already come. 'Tis grace that brought me safe thus far, and grace will lead me home." Hope is built on the record of God's faithfulness to us.

In a psalm which I read for today we have this word: "The day is thine; the night also is thine." We can remind ourselves of that truth when the night seasons come. Dark and light are the same with Him, and He is always ready to help us in our need.

Anchors hold the ship in place when necessary. St. Paul speaks of the great storm which overtook the ship he was in on his way to Rome. Everything was black and threatening. But he says, "They let out four anchors from the stern [of the ship] and prayed for day to come." (Acts 27:29). This book offers some anchors for your soul and mine. The more we anchor ourselves to the living God, the brighter hope will become.

In another place St. Paul says, "Hope does not disappoint us, because God's love has been poured into our hearts through the Holy Spirit which has been given to us." (Romans 5:5) Since He is the source and ground of our hope, we can rely on it. May every reader of this book find hope newly kindled day by day.

A Living Hope

And we rejoice in the hope of the glory of God. Not only so, but we also rejoice in our sufferings, because we know that suffering produces perseverance; perseverance, character; and character, hope. And hope does not disappoint us, because God has poured out His love into our hearts by the Holy Spirit, whom He has given us.

ROMANS 5:2B-5:5 (NIV)

My Grandparents Taught Me Many Things

How to dig for worms and how to fish
How to make kites and fly them
How to be generous
How to identify wild flowers and birds
How to appreciate some quality of character in most
everyone I meet
How to learn from and live with people from far-
away places
How to build model rockets
The value of learning—in or out of school
How to eat strange foods

Although my grandfather was the top executive at a large corporation, a typical good time with him involved a trip to what he called "Prosperity Mall"—a very small rundown general store in a very small rundown town in western Pennsylvania—to buy worms for a day of fishing for blue gills on the pond at the farm. Such a day would end with all of us sitting on the front porch swings at the red farmhouse, with all the lights out, listening to peepers in the pitch black.

There are two main reasons why I admire my grandparents so much. First, they have enjoyed giving generously to others, expecting nothing in return. In fact, though, they have received gifts of life-long friendships with people of all walks of life—farmers, business executives, auto mechanics, exchange students from around the world—who love them dearly.

Second, I think they've given me a clue about how to love my own children. Many think that real love means holding on to someone as tightly as possible. What I learned from them was just the opposite. They prepared their five children with the basic tools needed to face life responsibly. Then they said, "Go to it!" and let each kid go and do whatever he or she was interested in or enjoyed. They were proud of their kids, but didn't pressure them or demand anything from them. All five were very successful in the professions they chose, and, most importantly, they love my grandparents, as do all their grandchildren, and now great-grandchildren—far more than I have noticed in many families.

Last year, when my grandfather turned eighty, we had a party for him during which he gave a short speech summing up his first eighty years. It had three parts:

* What I'm Glad I Did (marry his wife and have five kids, buy a farm, travel)
* What I Wish I Had Done (learn to fly, learn to swim, learn a foreign language)
* What I Still Hope to Do (learn to use a computer, write a book on productivity, write a family history)

My grandparents, now both octogenarians as they enjoy calling themselves, are content because their lives have always been happily intertwined with their appreciation for new places and people and experiences. I hope that when I reach that age, I can look back over the years and be as happy as they are today.

Pam Jordan

Born Anew to a Living Hope

I Peter 1:3-9 and John 20:19-31

By His great mercy we have been born anew to a living hope through the resurrection of Jesus Christ from the dead, and to an inheritance which is imperishable, undefiled, and unfading, kept in heaven for you. . . I PETER 1:3B, 4 (RSV)

AT ITS BEST, LIFE IS INCOMPLETE. No matter how long we live, or how successful we may be in our chosen way of life, it still has an incompleteness about it. "We blossom and flourish as leaves on a tree, and wither and perish," says the hymn. And then it adds: "But naught changeth Thee."

And so, no matter who we are, we live by hope. Hope is a kind of invisible, inner quality which keeps us from despairing even when things are difficult. Peter is speaking to Christians in this text today. We know things were difficult for them, because later on he says, "Beloved, do not be surprised at the fiery ordeal which comes upon you to prove you, as though something strange were happening to you. But rejoice insofar as you share Christ's sufferings, that you may also rejoice and be glad when His glory is revealed." (I Peter 4:12, 13). Their lives were "on the line" every day because they believed in Jesus. If they had no hope, how could they carry on in the face of such trouble?

A dear and holy man of God in Yugoslavia whom I met last year spent two years in prison because of His loyalty to Jesus, and lost his hearing in one ear from the treatment he received there. Others have suffered in other ways. But all of them were sustained by "a living hope." They were ready to live faithfully, and if necessary, to die faithfully, because they were sustained by the hope God had placed in their hearts.

If we believe in God and in His Son Jesus Christ, the Holy Spirit plants "a living hope" in us, and that hope does not disappoint us! As a people we struggle daily with our feelings. Sometimes we feel depressed or sad, and are tempted to become bitter about life, because it has failed fully to satisfy us. God knows where you are, and He knows the desires that He has planted in your heart. He gave you hope for a life that will be full and complete when you invite Him to be your Lord and Savior. Do cherish that hope, dwell in it, and let it grow more intense as the days and years roll by.

Hope's Shining Ray   JANUARY 2

II Corinthians 4:13, 5:1 and Mark 3:20-35

So we do not lose heart.   II COR 4:16A (RSV)

PAUL SAYS, "OUR OUTWARD NATURE IS WASTING AWAY." We have only to look in the mirror and compare what we see there with a picture of ourselves fifteen or twenty years ago. For example, in my study, I have a picture of myself and my wife taken about a year after we were married. Friends who come in say that they recognize her but wouldn't know who I was if they weren't told! So much for our efforts to appear youthful. The wear and tear of the years do show! And yet there are also the lessons you have learned, problems you once faced that no longer trouble you. Life is not all creaking and groaning—even if our joints do creak at times.

Paul also says "our inner nature" is being made new day by day. What a tremendous truth! We do not live only for today. We are children of God, and we are on our way to something so much more wonderful than anything we have known: "eye hath not seen nor ear heard the things which God hath prepared for those who love Him." We are preparing to live in a new dimension—eternal life.

What our text says, then, is that as long as we live and breathe, we do not lose hope. There is no power on earth greater than God, and He has promised, "Lo I am with you always, even to the end of the age." How, then, can we lose hope, knowing that He will never put any burden on us greater than the strength

He gives us to bear it. We can rest in that, and rejoice in our hope.

And when we are called on to say goodbye to our loved ones for awhile, when death intervenes and takes them from us, we do not have to sorrow as those who have no hope. That is the time to renew our hope in the life everlasting, the life made possible by the love, the life, the death and resurrection of our Lord Jesus Christ. Our hope is eternal. Death cannot take it away. Sickness cannot rob us of it. Disappointment cannot steal it. Day by day, like Paul, our inner nature is being renewed. That does not grow old! So we do not lose heart!

Nevertheless, at Thy Word   JANUARY 3

Isaiah 6:1-8 and Luke 5:1-11

Master, we toiled all night and took nothing, but at Your word I will let down the nets. LUKE 5:5 (RSV)

I ALWAYS REMEMBER THIS VERSE as it appears in the King James version: "*Nevertheless*, at Thy word. . . ." Somehow that word "nevertheless" seems to catch the essence of this story for me.

Peter and his partners were at one of those times familiar to us all, when nothing seems to work. Our best intentions, our best efforts, our human skills—all amount to zero. Nothing. We may be resigned to this situation, or we may be terribly frustrated, but we simply do not know what to do next.

Many parents have faced situations like this. They have tried to teach their children what was right, they have tried to live as an example to them, and then they see them making wrong choices, harmful choices—perhaps even disastrous choices. And it's sometimes true even after our children are grown and away from home. We "have toiled all night and caught nothing!"

Then again, it may be our own situation or circumstances we cannot seem to change. All our best plans and wisdom don't seem to make a dent. We are stuck.

Jesus enters the story of Peter and his friends, and with a simple word directs them what to do. And that presents another problem. Will Peter do what the Master suggests, or will he persist in his own wisdom and experience? In this story Peter had only to believe and obey for everything to come out happily.

Jesus still enters the picture with us. He tells us to believe that "the battle is not done." He bids us place our problem on the altar before God and trust—hoping and *believing* that God can do that which we cannot do. He does not promise us that all will turn out just the way we would like. But He does promise that "all things work together for good to those who love God, to those who are called according to His purpose." Peter was asked to cast his net on the other side of the boat. Instead of casting our nets on the side of worry, scheming, fretting, nagging, controlling—we can cast them into the depths of the mercy of God. He *cannot* fail, because He is faithful!

Lord of the Valleys   JANUARY 4

Psalm 23 and John 10:22-30

Yea, though I walk through the valley of the shadow of death, I will fear no evil; for Thou art with me; Thy rod and Thy staff, they comfort me. PSALM 23:4 (KJV)

MOST OF OUR LIVES ARE LIVED, not on the mountaintops, but in the valleys of life. The Psalmist knew that life is not always lived by the quiet, peaceful stream of still waters. It has its difficult climbs and its steep valleys. There are times when conditions are so dark, so threatening, and so fearful that we cringe from going on. In *Pilgrim's Progress*, Bunyan tells us that when Christian got through the "Valley of Humiliation," he had to go through another valley, called the "Valley of the Shadow of Death." Just at the border of the valley, Christian met two men who had turned back. When Christian asked where they were going, they said, "Back! Back! We went as far as we dared." Christian asked what they had seen. "Why, the valley itself! It is dark as pitch, full of hobgoblins, satyrs and dragons, and fearful noise. There were clouds of confusion all over it; it is dreadful in every way."

This is Bunyan's way of describing those situations in life when we feel overwhelmed by circumstances beyond our control. But to get to the Celestial City, Christian had to go through the valley. There was no other route. And so it is with us. We cannot avoid the hard places, but God never sends us more than He gives us grace to bear. That is what Christian found as he made his way gingerly through the valley.

I suspect that your valleys are not different from mine. There are the unanswered questions about life's tragedies. There are the uncertainties about what the future might hold, and about our ability to meet them. A friend of mine who is fighting a serious physical condition said recently, "I don't think I mind dying. But I do not want to die *badly.*" He was concerned that his condition might become so bad that he would be unable to handle it.

But the Psalmist based his future hope on his past experience. I have a little card that I use as a Bible marker, and in beautiful lettering it reads, "We thank Thee for all that is past and we trust Thee for all that is to come."

Considering Our Sufferings   JANUARY 5

Romans 8:18-25 and Matthew 13:24-30 and 36-43

I consider that the sufferings of this present time are not worth comparing with the glory that is to be revealed to us. ROMANS 8:18 (RSV)

THIS SPRING SOME OF US read two books on suffering. One of them was by a philosophy professor, Peter Kreeft, and it was entitled, *Making Sense Out of Suffering*. The other book was by Elisabeth Elliot, whose missionary husband was killed by the Auca Indians in South America. It is entitled, *A Path Through Suffering*. In both cases the authors were addressing this age-old problem of suffering and our attitude toward it.

Our generation has been taught that we should not expect to suffer, nor should we have to suffer. There are those who now advocate that "euthanasia" (good death) be made available to people who don't want to suffer anymore.

And yet we all know that life is made up of suffering. Whether we believe in God or not, whether we *like it* or not, we are all going to suffer. Some of our suffering is in our thoughts and feelings. We experience grief and loss; we experience fears and disappointments. Some of us suffer from bodily aches and pains, uncertainty or declining physical health. It is the common lot of humankind.

This is where Paul speaks to us. He too had suffered but he kept his eye on something else: "the glory that is to be revealed to us"—an end to the struggle, an inner vision that something glorious lies ahead! As long as there is hope, which sends "a shining ray far down the future's broadening way," we can endure what we have to endure today.

I read recently these words: "Fear is always about what might happen next. It is never about what is happening now." I like that, and want to hold on to it the next time fear raises its ugly head in my thoughts. There is grace to deal with what's happening now, if we don't let fear of what might happen next interfere.

Paul is not asking us to "make light" of our sufferings as though they didn't exist. They do, and we all know it. But if we know that there is something worthwhile beyond the suffering, then we will find strength for what life brings.

Three Important Words

II Timothy 1:1-14 and Luke 17:5-10

*I am not ashamed, for I know whom I have believed and I am
persuaded that He is able to keep that which I have committed
unto Him . . .* II TIMOTHY 1:12 (KJV)

THESE THREE STATEMENTS ARE IMPORTANT, because they are
vital considerations for every one of us.

First Paul says, "I have believed." That's a simple enough
statement, but it's the foundation on which Paul had built his
life. He had believed in God. He had believed in the truthfulness
of God's promises made to Abraham and all his forefathers.
When Jesus revealed Himself to Paul on the Damascus Road,
Paul believed in Him. He started living for something new and
wonderful—living for Jesus. He believed and that made the
difference.

The next thing he says is "I know *whom* I have believed."
Too many people waste their lives by believing in the wrong
thing. They believe that job, family, money, activity, or possessions bring happiness and meaning to life. And what happens if
they are taken away? Does life lose its meaning then? Paul
knew whom he had put his faith in. As the years went by, he
knew Him better and better. Jesus had always been faithful.
Jesus had never failed him. So he could say, "I know." So can
we. The years only bring greater and greater assurance that
Jesus Christ is faithful.

Finally he says, "I am persuaded that He is able to keep that
which I have committed to Him." Believing leads to a kind of
knowledge. Experience helps us to know whom we have believed.
And experience then enables us to look forward with hope and
trust, being persuaded that God will not fail us in the future.

Whatever may come into our experience, we can be confident that He will be with us, and His grace will be sufficient for
our need. It is a great joy to write these words, because they are

true for each one of us. I encourage you to strengthen your faith in His all-sufficient love and mercy.

Looking in the Wrong Place   JANUARY 7

I Corinthians 15:19-26 and Luke 24:1-12

While [the women] were perplexed about this, behold two men stood by them in dazzling apparel, and as they were frightened and bowed their faces to the ground, the men said to them, "Why do you seek the living among the dead?" LUKE 24:4, 5 (RSV)

NO WONDER THE WOMEN WERE FRIGHTENED. Three days before, they had watched their Lord hanging dead on the cross. Besides not knowing whether they were in much danger, they had their greatest hopes shattered. All that was left to them was to come to the tomb for love's last rites.

Now two strange, dazzling figures stood before them. We can understand their fear. Then comes the disarming question: "Why do you seek the living among the dead?" They could have replied, "What do you mean, 'the living'? We have come to anoint our dead Lord for the grave."

Jesus had told them over and over that He would rise from the grave. But the starkness of death was so real that it seemed the only reality. It is often the same with us. We sing the hymns, say the prayers, and truly *want* to believe. But as the starkness of our situation tyrannizes us, we begin to think we see the only reality. We need to listen again to the angels' words: Why do you seek the living among the dead?

This question means I must stop looking in the wrong places for the answers to life's puzzles. I must cease looking down as I plod through life, and look up at the stars so that my horizons can be broadened. Life is more than the humdrum daily grind. There is a life of faith, trust, and love that has been made possible by the wonderful fact of the Resurrection.

Jesus Christ is really alive, and He has not gone out of business! I can choose to believe that and look for answers to my problems from Him. Or, I can keep looking in the dusty corners of yesterday, of broken hopes and shattered dreams—and mourn the loss of what can no longer be. If I believe in the reality of Jesus' resurrection, then there is a promise of new life for me.

I invite you to join me in a new resolution to seek life, to look forward, to build on faith rather than fear. Christ is risen! Alleluia!

The Still Small Voice   JANUARY 8

I Kings 19:9-14, Galatians 3:23-29, Luke 9: 18-24

. . . And after the fire a still small voice.
I KINGS 19:12B (RSV)

HAVING WON A DRAMATIC DECISIVE VICTORY against the false priests of Baal worship, Elijah ran away from Queen Jezebel who was determined to kill him. On Mount Horeb, Elijah hid in a cave. He felt exhausted, defeated, and utterly cast down. And then the word of the Lord came to him: "What are you doing here?" Elijah went over his tale of woe. "I have been very jealous for the Lord; the people have forsaken His covenant, gone over to the Baals, killed the Lord's prophets, and I—even I only, am left, and they are seeking my life, too."

He was told to get out of his hiding place, and to seek what God would do. "And the Lord passed by." The mountains shook, the rocks broke in pieces, wind howled, earthquake and fire followed. But none of these remarkable phenomena spoke to Elijah's condition. And still he waited. Then it happened. In the quiet that followed, "a still small voice." When Elijah wrapped his face in his mantle and listened, he heard God's message. Elijah was not alone. There were others who loved and served God, too. And God had important things (in God's plan) that Elijah still had to do.

Do you ever find yourself in a cave of self-pity, or of fear, hiding from the things that seem to threaten your security? It's easy just to withdraw inwardly, where no one can get to you. We withdraw from hurt, from people with whom we are angry or from situations we feel keenly disappointed about. But the question eventually comes to us, as it did to Elijah: What are you doing there? Are you ready to hear some new word, see some new evidence that God is God and that He is active in your life? Are you ready to go out of the cave and meet Him?

He wants to speak to us in that voice so small and still that we will miss it in the hurried bustle of life. He has things to speak to our heart—words of encouragement, hope, and direction. Listen, oh listen in your heart for that still, small voice!

One Who Intercedes   JANUARY 9

I John 2:1-6

We have an advocate with the Father, Jesus Christ the Righteous.
I JOHN 2:1B (RSV)

TODAY'S EPISTLE TALKS ABOUT accusation, guilt, and defense. The accusation is that we have sinned against the majesty and law of God. Our Judge is not a human being in black robes. He is none other than the Creator Himself, who knows our thoughts even before we think them. The guilt is ours. This verse refers to one who is guilty before being tried. Who is to defend such a one before the holy Judge of all? The answer: "We have an advocate, Jesus Christ the Righteous." Here we are face to face with the tender mercy of God, who has provided the Advocate for the guilty ones.

The Advocate takes our case before the Eternal Judge. Yes, the sinner is guilty. There can be no denying that. But the price has already been paid. What is the price? "*He* is the propitiation for our sins, and not for ours only, but also for the sins of the whole world." (verse 2) "Father, the sinner is wrong. He has not lived up to what You created Him to be. He has violated his own conscience, broken Your law, acted in selfish, foolish ways. He has even tried to convince himself that he isn't wrong. But Father, I died for him. All my righteousness I offer in the place of his wrongness. Look upon that, Father, and forgive."

That is not the same plea that earthly lawyers make. They may try to prove the prisoner innocent, or convince the judge that no one can *prove* him guilty, but he does not offer to take the punishment for him. Only God does that. Justice and mercy have kissed each other, and mercy has triumphed over justice!

Jesus Christ assures us that He will forgive us and cleanse us. We do not have to be burdened with past mistakes—however serious they may have been. He says that He will remember them no more. There is peace of heart in the forgiveness of God!

Remembering and Rejoicing   JANUARY 10

Deuteronomy 26:1-11 and Luke 4:1-13

And you shall rejoice in all the good which the Lord your God has given to you and your house. . . .   DEUT. 26:11 (RSV)

SOMEONE RECENTLY SAID, "We do not rejoice enough in God's small victories." She meant we need to see and respond to the *little things* by which God advances His purposes and shows His power. While we wait for the *big events*, we may be missing countless small ones that are meant to build up our faith and strengthen our relationship with our heavenly Father.

Why were the Israelites to rejoice? They were to remember their cruel slavery in Egypt. They were to remember that God had heard their cries and sent a deliverer to lead them into a land of promise and freedom.

Then they were to remember the wilderness in which they wandered. There were thousands of them and their situation was impossible, humanly speaking. Yet God fed them with manna and kept them through all their trials.

Rejoicing was not something they could just do if they wished. They were *commanded* to rejoice because rejoicing was a proper response to what they had received.

You and I are also called to rejoice. Remembering back to former years, we find many happy memories, gifts, and blessings bestowed on us along our pilgrimage. Faces come back to mind of those who have loved us and done us good. But their memory should be a blessing—not an occasion for sadness or self-pity. We do them no honor if we give in to the selfish indulgence of bitterness. Birthdays and holidays should be times of thanksgiving, not of maudlin vain regrets.

Of course, some memories still have a bitter taste about them—mistakes, sins, wrongs we have done to others, little or great. We cannot change the past, but we can accept the grace of forgiveness and let the past be done. The memories of past sins can flood us with new thankfulness for the wonder and miracle of God's forgiving grace.

Along with memories and rejoicing in past and present blessings, we have the blessed assurance that the future is in the same loving Hand. We do not know what the future holds, but as we remember and rejoice, we can strengthen our faith that "nothing shall be able to separate us from the love of God which is in Christ Jesus our Lord."

Behold, What Manner of Love JANUARY 11

I John 3:1-7 and Luke 24: 35-48

Behold, what manner of love the Father hath bestowed on us, that we should be called the sons of God . . . Beloved, now are we the sons of God. I JOHN 3:1A, 2A (KJV)

THE OLDER I GET, THE MORE SURPRISED I AM by the goodness of the love of God. The more I look back on the wasted opportunities, the mistakes I have made, the wrong choices and wrong attitudes, the more amazing seems God's great love.

Our human love is so limited. Do you find that you have to fight the feelings of anger and even vindictiveness when the people you love hurt you? Although you know that you do love them, when they neglect you or hurt your feelings, it is hard not to feel some bitterness towards them.

God's love is different. We know that He is grieved and injured by the rebellion and sin in the world. How it must grieve His great heart to see the amount of havoc wreaked on helpless people by evil and selfishness. Yet He does not cease to love, even those whom we would call enemies. Not only does He show His love towards all humanity by the death of His Son on the cross, He also invites those who have been His enemies to become His sons. That's who we were, when we walked in our own ways and followed our own plans.

As I said, the older I get, and the less time I know I have to "do something great," or to change myself into something better, the more my wonder grows, that this love, so great, so infinite, so filled with hope, is for me.

God's Unending Supply   JANUARY 12

I Kings 17:1-16 and Mark 12:38-44

And the barrel of meal wasted not, neither did the
cruse of oil fail, according to the word of the Lord,
which He spake by Elijah.   I KINGS 17:16 (KJV)

THERE ARE STORIES IN THE BIBLE THAT demonstrate the great truth: God is greater than His creation and He is Lord of all natural law. The widow of Zarephath showed her faith in God by sacrificing her meager supply of food to share with the prophet and was blessed. Another example of this is the story of the Feeding of the Five Thousand in the Gospels.

Corrie ten Boom told a similar story years ago, one that happened during her confinement in a Nazi camp. They had managed to smuggle in a small bottle of vitamin C, and Corrie's sister, Betsy, among others, was desperately ill. Day after day drops of the precious vitamin were given and the bottle did not run dry! God's faithfulness and power are unending.

The truth of these stories should be part of our daily life. God's resources are limitless. His supply does not run out, and they are available to us if we want them badly enough. There is always enough grace for today's need. His mercies are new every morning. His love took Jesus all the way to the cross, and the Bible says, "He who spared not His own Son, but freely gave Him up for us all, how shall He not also freely give us all things with Him?"

Are we claiming His inner resources for the problems we face daily? He will surprise us with new mercies. He will give us strength when we have none of our own—because He is God and because He loves us.

If we know, even in a limited way, that His grace is sufficient, and that His strength is made perfect in our weakness, then we have enough to claim what we need today from His unending supply.

The Good Shepherd JANUARY 13

I John 3:16-24 and John 10:11-18

*I am the Good Shepherd; I know my own and my own know me
. . . and I lay down my life for the sheep.* JOHN 10:14, 15B (RSV)

THAT WORD "SHEPHERD" HAS COME OVER into the Christian
church as the word "pastor." The dictionary says that a
pastor is a herdsman or a caretaker. We even call the members
of a church "the pastor's flock." So we have some understanding of what "shepherd" means when Jesus speaks of it.

He is the *good* Shepherd. They tell us that a good shepherd
knows each one of his sheep. They are not just "things," they
are individuals. Surely that's what Jesus is saying to us when he
says, "I know my own." It was said of former Speaker of the
House of Representatives, Thomas P. "Tip" O'Neill, that no
matter how powerful or successful he became, he always
remembered his old friends and neighbors. He called them by
name. And they loved and respected him for it.

How much more should we love the Lord of heaven and
earth, the Good Shepherd, who knows us personally and calls us
by name. "I know my own," He says. The children sing about a
Santa, "who knows when you are sleeping," etc., but we sing
about a Shepherd who knows and cares—and is always with us!

Then He says that His sheep know Him. Do we really
know Him? We're getting acquainted as years go on. We may
have neglected learning to know Him, but most of us know
Him better than we realize. We know Him as He comes to us
in our need. We know Him as He answers prayers, not always
giving us what we want! And learning to know Him, we are
learning to trust Him. His ways are not our ways. "Perverse
and foolish, oft I strayed, but yet in love He sought me." That's
how we're coming to know the Good Shepherd—who can
always be trusted to care, who lays down His life for His
sheep—for you and me.

We Would See Jesus   JANUARY 14

Philippians 3:12-21 and Matthew 21:33-43

. . . Because Christ Jesus has made me His own.
PHILIPPIANS 3:12B (RSV)

M Y BROTHER DIED AT THE YOUNG AGE OF FIFTY-SIX. His
had not been a happy life. His marriage had failed, many
jobs came and went, and finally he succumbed to lung cancer.
Before he died, however, he was visited by a minister who
wanted to help him face death with hope. At that point, my
brother could not speak because of an apparatus in his throat
to help him breathe. But he could write. So he wrote on his pad,
"All my life I have been looking for something." The minister
responded, "It was Jesus, wasn't it?" My brother nodded,
"Yes." I am happy to report that he found peace at the last, and
by faith saw Jesus as the answer to his longing.

Is life a disappointment to you, and do you find yourself
unfulfilled with your lot? Many, many people are, especially
when life deals us a hard blow—sickness, infirmity, disable-
ment, and the like. The loss of those we have held dear can be
a big hurdle and readjustment. But the question still lingers: is
Jesus there with you?

What keeps us from seeing Him in our everyday circumstances?—our own stubbornness, feelings such as bitterness,
resentments, unforgiveness, and fear of the future. These things
can simply blot out an awareness of His blessed and loving
presence. I know from my own experience the difference
between living in these feelings and looking for and recognizing
Jesus' presence in my life. The difference is one between night
and day.

Jesus says, "If anyone opens the door, I will come into him
and eat with him, and he with me." (Rev. 3:20) What He wants
from every one of us is our love and trust. Out of that everything good can grow.

Paul says, "I press forward to make it [the resurrection] my own, because Christ Jesus has made me His own." He has already claimed you, loved you, lived for you, and died for you. Now He wants you to *see* Him at work within your heart and within the circumstances of your life today.

Prayer

O Lord, grant me heavenly wisdom, that I may learn above all things to seek and to find Thee; above all things to relish and to love Thee; and to perceive of all other things as being what indeed they are, at the disposal of Thy wisdom; through Jesus Christ our Lord. Amen.

Adapted from Thomas à Kempis

On That Day JANUARY 15

Isaiah 25:6-9 and John 20:1-18

It will be said on that day, "Lo, this is our God; we have waited for Him, that He might save us." ISAIAH 25:9 (RSV)

THE PEOPLE OF ISRAEL LIVED BY HOPE, the hope of God's intervention and salvation. Sometimes they almost lost hope; but when historical, political and military situations darkened, there was always a flame of hope that God would not abandon His people and would not forget His promise.

When the old Simeon in the temple met Mary and Joseph with the infant Jesus, he said simply, "Lord, now let your servant depart in peace, for my eyes have seen Your salvation." He recognized that Jesus was the fulfillment of those promises and the spiritual hope they inspired.

The disciples went through many ups and downs with Jesus. Sometimes they thought they understood what He was saying, but then they would lose sight of it. Even faithful Peter denied Him three times the night He was arrested and tried.

We, too, have our ups and downs in following Jesus. Things are not always clear and easy to understand. We are "cast down" by some of the things that happen to us, and we may even grow very discouraged and begin to lose hope. If such is your case, I want to bid you to remember that The Day of Resurrection is not a myth, a fanciful tale. It is a reality so great, so wonderful that we can hardly express it. Jesus said, "Because I live, you will live also." That does not mean merely existing. It means living, with all that living can and should mean.

When there are times you are called on to bear some irksome limitation or some pain, He lives for you and you can experience His reality—by a simple act of child-like faith.

Yes, "On that day it will be said, "Lo, this is our God; we have waited for Him, that He might save us." That day is here—for you and me.

Blessed is the Man   JANUARY 16

Psalm 1 and James 3:13-4:3

*Blessed is the man that walketh not in the counsel of the
ungodly, nor standeth in the way of sinners, nor sitteth in
the seat of the scornful. But his delight is in the law of the Lord;*
PSALM 1:1, 2A (KJV)

WHAT EXACTLY IS "THE COUNSEL OF THE UNGODLY"? The Psalmist assures us that the way to be blessed is to avoid walking in it.

One "ungodly" counsel today is that life is good only if it is at its peak. And so we have a society that does not value life itself, but only life that is productive. I shudder when I read what is happening to people in the Netherlands who are now subject to "the good death," sometimes at their doctors and relatives' judgment. In our mad pursuit of instant pleasure and relief from all suffering, we seem to be rushing to some very ungodly ideas about what life is all about.

A dear friend of mine from forty years ago has lived with pretty constant pain most of her adult life. She said jokingly once, "With my luck, I'll probably live to be a hundred." But she has maintained not only a stalwart faith that life is good in spite of pain, but she has matured spiritually through it, and has been a great encouragement to others.

Another "ungodly" counsel is that when we get to the point where we can no longer do the work which once occupied much of our time and energy, that we are of no use. In England, they use the term "redundant" to refer to people who are no longer needed in certain jobs and have to be "laid off." Redundant, according to my thesaurus, means superfluous, unnecessary. What a way to categorize any human life! Some of the most blessed and important relationships I have ever known were with people who were shut-in, disabled or otherwise "retired." Their spirit and their wisdom were all the more available to me, and I count myself blessed indeed to have been able to know them.

Let us never walk in the counsel of the ungodly, believing that life is only good "at its peak." It is good in the valleys, too, because it is the gift of God. Not only so, but God uses those valleys to draw us away from the things that pass away, that we may set our hearts on the things that are eternal—His love, His goodness, and His tender mercies.

A People of Hope   JANUARY 17

Ephesians 2:11-22 and Mark 6:30-44

Remember that you were at that time separated from Christ . . .
having no hope and without God in the world. But now, in
Christ Jesus you who once were far off have been brought near
in the blood of Christ.   EPH. 2:12, 13A (RSV)

WE CHRISTIANS HAVE BEEN BROUGHT from hopelessness (without Christ) to a living hope (in Christ). We cannot live as though the only thing that matters is the present life.

But if we have lived beyond the natural "halfway point" of our lives, we know that life is meant to be more than eating, drinking and making merry. Those things are fine in their place, but they do not give life its true meaning. Life is not hastening to a meaningless bottomless pit. Jesus did not come and die on the cross for that. He came to give us hope beyond the day-to-day dreariness which life can sometimes become.

That hope is that we shall live anew in the presence of God. So our task and calling now is to live in hope. Discouragement and despair are enemies of hope. They are products of self-pity and lack of faith. There is plenty of reason to believe in the goodness and mercy of God since he has already proved His faithfulness again and again for each of us. Standing on that ground, we can nourish hope.

This is not an easy hope that things will just get better, or that we won't have to have aches and pains. It is not even hope that we won't experience sorrow and grief. It is a surer, firmer, better hope. It is the hope that life has been worthwhile. That God is in charge. That He is leading us—sometimes through sunny days, sometimes through shadows. But He is leading us—home where we shall see Him, and be with Him *forever.* What more could we hope for?

He Preached the Good News   January 18

Philippians 4:4-7 and Luke 3:7-18

So with many other exhortations, he [John the Baptist]
preached good news to the people.   LUKE 3:18 (RSV)

Have no anxiety about anything   PHIL. 4:6A (RSV)

TODAY WE SEE THE CHRISTIAN FAITH AND the Christian way
of life openly mocked, scoffed at, and ridiculed—in magazines, newspapers, and on TV. Immorality is openly treated as
normal in a society that has decided that the Church does not
have any "Good News" for it.

We cannot change the way the world perceives our message.
But a more relevant question is, How do we perceive God's
message to us? Is it good news? Will it nourish and sustain and
strengthen us for every kind of experience we have in life or do
we relegate the Gospel to sentimentality like a scrapbook full of
pictures and memories—to be taken out now and then, but
then put away and forgotten?

John the Baptist's message sounds severe and demanding.
But it was really a message of hope. God had not forgotten His
people. God's kingdom was ready to break in upon them and
he called people to get ready for it.

Our message is the same. God's rule is at the point of coming into our lives whenever we are willing to open our hearts to
him. He is ready to break in, to take charge of our lives, to
assume the responsibility of seeing to it that we have all the
grace and help we need for anything that comes. What a strong
word of encouragement!

Paul wrote from his Roman prison to his friends at Philippi,
"Have no anxiety about anything." Speak to God about all
your needs thanking Him for what He has already done and
believe that He will give you what you need each moment of
your life.

The old anxious thoughts will keep coming back. Keep

turning those thoughts over to Him. He is with you, to take them from you. He is greater than the things we worry about, and if we keep on turning to Him we will find peace—the peace that passes all understanding!

Beneath His Guiding Hand   JANUARY 19

Joel 2:21-27 and Matthew 6:25-33

Fear not, O land; be glad and rejoice; for the Lord will do great things.   JOEL 2:21 (KJV)

I AM REMINDED OF THE GREAT DEBT we owe to those who came to this country and laid down its foundations in their firm belief in God. They had come as exiles from their native land. We are indeed a blessed nation, and our history cannot be understood apart from its spiritual foundations. Yet, I fear, we are in danger of losing that today—this sense of connection with those who built this country. We can see that our leaders are often lacking in great vision, and many times led more by personal ambition than real concern for the country. There does not seem to be much we can do about it, for most of us are limited in our ability to change the present course of things. There is, however, one weapon we can wield. There is one task we can perform, and it may be the most important of all: we can pray for our country and for its leaders. God is still God, and He can overrule kings and counsellors—presidents, secretaries, senators, congressmen—the lot! Our weapons are spiritual, and if we will use them, we can be part of His saving work in steering this country in the right path.

There is another dimension also in which we need to be involved for the good of our nation. The prophet Joel wrote in a time when his country had been laid waste and was under the domination of others. The key, however, to their deliverance was what happened inside them. "Turn to me with all your heart . . . and rend your heart and not your garments, and turn unto the Lord your God; for He is gracious and merciful, slow to anger and of great kindness . . ." (Joel 2:12,13) That is still true today, and although we may think we are not the problem, yet God calls every one of us to turn to Him with all our heart.

Let us give thanks for all the blessings we have received, and remember especially our beloved land. God still means good, as our text assures us. "We give thanks for all that is past; and we trust Him for all that is to come."

Two Keywords for Peace   JANUARY 20

Mark 1:14-20 and I Cor. 7: 29-31

Jesus came to Galilee. . . . "repent ye and believe in the gospel."
MARK 1:14 (KJV)

I TALK FREQUENTLY WITH A WOMAN WHO DOES NOT seem to know just what she wants, but she never fails to express her abiding and implacable anger at God. She continuously rehearses her case against God. She says she has done everything to deserve God's blessing and does not receive it, while "others" have done nothing to deserve it, yet they have it.

This dear soul has missed the keywords to peace. Those words are included in today's text, where the Evangelist sums up Jesus' preaching in one verse. Jesus, he says, came preaching the kingdom of God, saying "Repent and believe in the gospel." Those are the key words. Repent. Believe. And strange as it may seem, you don't really have one without the other.

Our woman insists that she is innocent and misunderstood—by God. What she misses is that we all fall short of the glory of God. We have many feelings and motives inside us which are basically selfish—and therefore we need to repent. Repentance is turning from what we know ourselves to be, seeking to change toward what we are meant to be. If we refuse to repent, we cut ourselves off from the blessings God has for us in forgiveness and grace.

The second keyword is "believe." When our hearts are hardened by disappointments, sad circumstances, or even by fear of what the future might hold, we may cry out at what seems to be the unfairness of it all. But if we will believe the Gospel, "the good news," that God's kingdom is truly at hand and that He is with us in the midst for whatever circumstance we face, then we can find peace, even in a storm. Even though it doesn't always look that way to us, Jesus Christ says that the kingdom of God is at hand. He laid down His own life to usher that kingdom in. When God brought Him forth from the tomb, He set His seal on all Jesus had said and done. So we can believe His word, for it is true. He came to make it possible for us to be children of that kingdom, children of God. Repenting and believing—these are the key words to entering the kingdom and daily living in it.

I Press on to Make it My Own   JANUARY 21

Philippians 3:12-21 and Matthew 21:33-43

Not that I have already obtained this or am already perfect;
but I press on to make it my own, because Christ Jesus
has made me His own. PHIL. 3:12 (RSV)

PAUL IS TALKING HERE ABOUT THE UNFINISHED LIFE, the uncompleted process in which he is a willing participant. He is not flinching from his difficult circumstances.

We need to hear this word, because when life throws something at us that is so hard to bear we hardly know how we are going to get through it, there is a deadly temptation to resign, to withdraw from the struggle. Too many people die inside before their body gives up the battle. Our bodies would be happier with us if we began to struggle against hopelessness and despair!

Paul looks forward to seeing Jesus, to sharing in the resurrection. He sees his life as an ongoing commitment to become more and more what the Creator intended it to be. When he wound up in Caesar's prison, his great missionary zeal and urgent sense of call to proclaim the Gospel to the whole world must have been very frustrated! But there's no pessimism in this letter. It is full of concern for others and thankfulness for the small favors people have shown him, and fairly bursts with deep optimism and hope.

Recently when undergoing several medical tests, I found out how quickly we can become absorbed in our physical condition! Yet through every dark uncertainty, we have the assurance that God is with us, that His grace is sufficient, and that we are being beckoned forward. What lies ahead is the fulfillment of life, the purpose for which we were created—if we press on to make it our own. God's grace does not bid us be passive; God's peace does not mean the end of struggle. Rather, in the midst of uncertainty about the future, we are to press on. Jesus is our sure reward if we put our trust in Him and persevere to the end. He not only accompanies us through every trial, but He waits in morning brightness to greet us when the journey is over.

So, then, with Paul, let us say, "I have not already obtained this [all that God has for us], nor am I already perfect. But I press on to make it my own."

I Must Stay at Your House Today JANUARY 22

II Thessalonians 1: 5-12 and Luke 19:1-10

"Zaccheus, make haste and come down; for I must stay at your house today." LUKE 19:5B (RSV)

MOST OF US ENJOY THIS LITTLE INCIDENT WITH Zaccheus, because he seems so human, and we see a side of Jesus that makes Him, too, seem very human.

Notice that although Zaccheus was eager to *see* Jesus, it

was Jesus who initiated the visit. It is important to see how eager Jesus was to have the visit with this despised, hated tax collector.

It would be very reassuring to all of us to remember that Jesus is equally eager to stay at our house today. The final verse in the Gospel today says, "For the Son of man came to seek and to save the lost." His mission on earth was to find abiding places in the hearts of those who would receive Him. It is a part of the mysterious mercy of God that He desires to dwell with us.

The second thing I notice is how happy Zaccheus was when he realized that Jesus was willing to go to his home. "He made haste and came down and received Him joyfully." In my own life, I can truthfully say that receiving Jesus into the home of my heart has brought me deep joy. It doesn't mean that I have always been happy, or that things have always been easy. But as the years go on, I am more and more grateful that He has been willing to come and abide with me.

When Jesus came into Zaccheus's life, it made a difference. Suddenly Zaccheus found himself ready to deal with the wrong areas of his life. He became aware of his responsibilities as a neighbor, a child of God. "Half my goods I give to feed the poor." He was willing, too, to look at the places he had been wrong. "If I have defrauded anyone of anything, I restore it fourfold." That was as radical a change as you could imagine.

When Jesus comes into our lives, He never leaves us the way He finds us. So everyone who invites Him into his heart and home finds that He begins the process of changing us. It is not a negative thing, but a very hopeful one. Since none of us is yet perfect, it is wonderful to know that the process is going on!

Forgive Our Foolish Ways   January 23

Matthew 4:12-17 and I Corinthians 15:1-11

From that time Jesus began to preach, saying, "Repent, for the
Kingdom of heaven is at hand."   Matt. 4:17 (RSV)

BEGINNING WITH HIS BAPTISM JESUS COMES on to the public
scene with the message, "The Kingdom of God is at hand;
repent and believe in the gospel." (Mark 1:14b, 15)

Because God love us, and because His best can come only as
we get rid of the things that stand in the way of receiving His
best, we have to be called to repentance over and over again. It
is never just a call to change by our own effort. We are never
required to "climb the steps of heaven" by our own pains and
in our own strength. We would never make it! The call to repent
is always joined with the call to "believe in the gospel," which
means, "believe in the good news." It is always a positive invitation, because whatever change we need to make, that change is
possible by the grace of God.

Looking out the window in February, we can see the length-
ening daylight. Spring isn't here yet (not in New England, at
least!) but it *is* coming. Before many weeks, flowers will emerge
from their winter's sleep, trees will put forth leaves and blossoms,
and the earth will be adorned with new signs of life. We *expect*
that because we trust God's faithfulness. In the same way, you
can believe that God is at work in you to bring some wonderful
change. We can turn from defeat and hopelessness to faith and
trust. Jesus came to this earth, gave His life, died and rose again
that it might be so. Nothing can keep it from happening if we
"repent and believe in the gospel." We, too, can change!

It Shall Come to Pass JANUARY 24

Isaiah 2:1-5 and Matthew 24:36-44

It shall come to pass in the latter days that the mountain of the house of the Lord shall be established as the highest of the mountains . . . and all nations shall flow to it. ISAIAH 2:2 (RSV)

SOME OF THE MOST DISAPPOINTING THINGS that have ever happened to any of us are unfulfilled expectations and broken promises. Parents have to be careful not to "set up" their children with false promises, that they will not, or cannot, fulfill.

It happens in this life that we cannot always do what we thought we could. Things do change, and we have to change with them. In my case, it turned out better than if things had gone the way I had expected them, but I was slow to see that.

Do we have an attitude of suspicion in our relationship with the Lord? Or do we really expect that "it shall come to pass" as He has promised? When Jesus first appeared on this earth, few people were still clinging to the prophetic promise which foretold His coming. There was just a small band of faithful souls who chose to believe that it would come to pass as God had foretold. In Luke's Gospel, Elizabeth says to Mary, "Blessed is she who believed that there would be a fulfillment of what was spoken to her from the Lord." (Luke 1:45) Anyone who clings to that faith is bound to be blessed!

What is it that God is promising? That He will ultimately have His way, that victory belongs to the Crucified One, that we who put our trust in Him *cannot* ultimately be disappointed of our hope. "It shall come to pass."

Our faith needs to grow in the midst of delayed fulfillment. Our faith needs to be purified as we get disappointed in our *human* expectations. We can wait, watch and find more than we hoped—if we choose to believe "it shall come to pass."

Blessings and Woes   JANUARY 25

And He [Jesus] lifted His eyes on His disciples, and said,
"Blessed are you poor, for yours is the kingdom of God."
LUKE 6:20 (RSV)

THE "BEATITUDES" TURN THINGS UPSIDE DOWN. They are a catalog of the conditions that Jesus calls "Blessed," which could also be translated "Happy," or "Fortunate." We could agree, could we not, that the world still doesn't believe it. Only those with ears to hear and hearts to understand can enter into the mystery of these words.

Jesus was addressing conditions that really existed. Most of his hearers were "poor," literally—not figuratively. They were the common people. And Paul reminds the Christians in Corinth, "Not many of you were wise by worldly standards, not many were powerful, not many were of noble birth . . . God chose what is low and despised in the world . . ." (I Cor. 1:26, 28) They *were* poor. Some of them were hungry. Many of them had griefs—loss of dear ones, and so on. We know that Jesus was not saying that these things were enjoyable, and we are instructed by him elsewhere to care for those who are in need. So what is He saying?

If your condition is one of natural sadness, or leads to worry and anxiety, He calls you to look beyond the moment. "Yours is the kingdom of God." Into the midst of your need God comes with faith and hope that no earthly condition can destroy. One of the hostages who had been held in Lebanon for many years wrote that he was sustained through the most brutal suffering by the belief that God was with him, and that God would finally prevail over all the forces of evil. That faith was stronger than the suffering he had to undergo.

Whatever your circumstance, remember that God is waiting to give you His best: the kingdom, satisfaction, even laughter. As one writer, says, "O taste and see that the Lord is good. Blessed are those who take refuge in Him."

That You May Believe   JANUARY 26

Acts 4:32-35 and John 20: 19-31

*Now Jesus did many other signs in the presence of His disciples,
which are not written in this book. But these are written—that
you may believe that Jesus is the Christ, the Son of God, and that
believing you may have life in His Name.* JOHN 20:30, 31 (RSV)

EASTER ALWAYS BRINGS OUR MINDS TO ETERNAL THINGS. As
we rehearse the story of Jesus' last days on earth, the sorrow of His disciples when He was crucified, their shattered
hopes and bewilderment, we then can share their inexpressible
joy when they discovered that He was risen from the dead! It is
this bright and joyful hope that brings throngs into the churches on Easter, because something in us responds to the Good
News that Death does not have the final word.

But does the joy remain? Do we go on from the beauty of
Easter into the new life that the living Lord offers us? Not if we
slip back into our old thought patterns, full of doubt, fear, self-
pity, and unbelief. If we allow these enemies of our souls to
remain, we lose hold of the very beauty and joy we felt in the
glad Easter celebration.

Spring around us bids spring awaken within us. "All the
winter of our sins, long and dark is flying, from His light to
whom we give laud and praise undying." (From a hymn by St.
John of Damascus, eighth-century). Year after year Easter
comes and goes. Will we let it change us, lift us up to a new
level of faith and hope, or let it pass as just another church festival? It's up to us.

John wrote His Gospel for people like us. He knew the importance of believing, and that *life*, true life, is found in our faith in
Jesus Christ, the living Son of God. The glow of Easter is still with
us. Its light still shines, and its beauty appears in the flowers and
trees. Let us join the millions of others who have "come to
believe," and who experience new life through their faith in Him.

The Spirit Gives Life   JANUARY 27

Psalm 103 and II Corinthians 3:1-6

For the written code kills, but the Spirit gives life.
II COR. 3:6 (RSV)

TOO MANY CHRISTIANS ARE PHARISEE CHRISTIANS. The Pharisee Christian went into the temple to pray and thanked God that he was not like the ungodly people around him. He was proud of his moral uprightness and his spiritual credentials. Jesus said that the Pharisee already had his reward and couldn't expect anything else from God. On the other hand, the publican was so keenly aware of how far short he had come that all he could do was smite his breast and say, "God be merciful to me, a sinner." *That* man, said Jesus, went down to his house justified, forgiven.

Our relationship with God is not to be governed by trying to add up "merit badges" the way we used to do in the Boy Scouts. We are not to be lured into spiritual pride because of the good things we do or the bad things we do not do. This is a different kind of relationship. God's mercy and grace is the foundation of our faith—not our goodness nor our good works!

The letter of the law kills. Whenever we begin to chalk up virtues in ourselves we kill something inside us. We kill that tender, delicate part that is sensitive to others, willing to see when we are wrong, open to the gentle moving of the Holy Spirit. We should so treasure and value this tender part of our hearts that we are wary of the temptation to think too highly of ourselves. The Spirit gives life. That's what we really want, isn't it? Abundant, flowing life, like a running brook, springs in the dry moments of life that burst forth unexpectedly. Life in abundance! The Spirit gives life.

Don't get hung up on winning arguments, having right opinions, always doing the right thing (or worrying about doing the right thing). Don't waste time justifying yourself when you have made a mistake or are found to be wrong. Just let the Spirit give you more life day by day.

All Things New   JANUARY 28

Acts 14:8-18, Revelation 21:1-6, and John 13:31-35

And He who sat upon the throne said, "Behold, I make
all things new." REVELATION 21:5A (RSV)

SOMETIMES WE DON'T FEEL VERY NEW. We wake up with the
same kinds of thoughts we had yesterday. We go through
familiar routines. It's easy to think everything will always be the
same—but it isn't.

Although we can't usually perceive it clearly, life isn't going
in circles. We're moving forward. We haven't completed our
journey, and we haven't yet become what we should be, or
want to be. But we *are* on our way.

Here in the next-to-last chapter of the Bible we hear the
Almighty God saying, "Behold I make all things new." This
verse speaks of a New Heaven and a New Earth—a renewed
creation that still awaits its perfect fulfillment. It's part of our
great Christian hope that this creation will not be abandoned,
but that in God's plan it will be made new. That's a wonderful
hope which awaits all of us who believe in Him.

But there is another meaning to this phrase. There is a newness here and now that God has for us as we cooperate with him.
We can have new thoughts, new attitudes about ourselves. We
can forgive ourselves for past sins and mistakes, knowing that
God has forgiven us already. We can forgive others for mistreat-
ing us because God has forgiven us and has given us the grace to
forgive. We can replace self-pity with concern for others. We can
look beyond our own cares and see where we can bring love to
others. We can do that whether we are at home or in a hospital
or other institution, for none of us is totally alone. God's newness
begins on the inside.

We may like our old routines and feel comfortable with our
old shoes—but no one cares for stale bread, warmed-over
potatoes, or wilting flowers. We like some things new. That's
where God's work comes in. It keeps us fresh. It puts a new

Spirit within. It helps us look up and see that though we still have problems, we have a loving Savior. He makes all things new—even those of us who are growing old. Newness after all is not a matter of age. It is a matter of spirit.

I mean to be one of God's "new ones," don't you?

The Year of the Lord's Favor JANUARY 29

Isaiah 61:1-4, and Luke 4:14-19

The Spirit of the Lord is on me, . . . to proclaim the year of the Lord's favor. LUKE 4:18A, 19 (NIV)

AFTER JESUS HAD STOOD UP IN THE SYNAGOGUE OF Nazareth and read these words early in his ministry, He said to the people: "Today this Scripture has been fulfilled in your hearing." (Luke 4:21) They formed the "blueprint" of Jesus' ministry on this earth—preaching good news to the poor, binding up the brokenhearted, proclaiming liberty to those who were bound, comforting the mourning, and proclaiming the "year of the Lord's favor."

It is a good verse to meditate on. For it is as true for us today as it was when the prophet first spoke it centuries ago.

God's favor rests upon each one of us. That may be hard to realize. But think, if you will, of the times you may have felt that His *disfavor* was toward you. I suspect many of us have, openly or secretly, entertained the thought that, for some reason, God was mad at us.

There is always a mystery in God's dealing with us. Sometimes His mercies are severe, and don't seem like mercies at all. Only later, looking back, can we see that the Hand which overshadowed us with grief or illness or tragedy of some kind was a Hand outstretched in love.

Here is a little verse I have treasured over the years:

> Child of My love, lean hard,
> And let Me feel the pressure of thy care;
> I know thy burden, child. I shaped it;
> Poised it in Mine own hand; made not proportion
> In its weight to thine unaided strength.
> For even as I laid it on, I said,
> "I shall be near, and while she leans on Me,
> This burden shall be Mine, not hers;
> So shall I keep My child within the circling arms
> Of my own love." Here lay it down, nor fear
> To impose it on a shoulder which upholds
> The government of worlds. Yet closer come:
> Thou art not near enough. I would embrace thy care;
> So I might feel My child reposing on My breast.
> Thou lovest Me? I knew it. Doubt not then;
> But loving Me, lean hard.
>
> *Author unknown*

So remember, it *is* the year of the Lord's favor—toward you and for you.

Saving and Losing   JANUARY 30

Isaiah 2:6-10 and Mark 8:34-38

Whoever would save his life will lose it, and whoever loses his life for my sake and the gospel's will save it.   MARK 8:35 (RSV)

THE SADDEST PEOPLE ARE THOSE WHO TRY TO "HOLD ON." Some cling to "things" as though that is the meaning of their life. One dear elderly lady was miserable, in spite of being well-off and having a lovely home—she was afraid of outlasting her resources! Some "hold on" to others, long after their death. Queen Victoria lived in mourning for sixty years after Prince Albert's death. Some people I have known refused to let go a loved one who had died, thus choosing a kind of death for themselves. Trying to "save" their life, they were losing it.

Some people seek to save their life by their stinginess. John D. Rockerfeller, Sr., used to throw dimes to people during the Depression. Yet near the end of his life he asserted he would give all he had to be able to live longer.

Jesus is talking about trying to hang on to control of our life at all costs. And He says if that's the way we're trying to save it, the cost is too high.

He makes a positive statement here, however—there *is* a way to save our lives: (1) Deny ourselves; (2) Take up our cross, and (3) Follow Him. He recognizes there is something in every one of us that we must deny in order to truly live. That self-denial is the refusal to give in to our selfish, vindictive, proud, and jealous selves.

The cross we are asked to take up is that of giving God permission to cross out those "selves" through whatever means He chooses. The cross may be working in you, crossing out things you would dearly love to hold on to. But if you recognize God's loving hand at work, you are taking up your cross and it is having its desired effect.

Following Jesus is more than praying or attending worship services. It is cultivating His company, conversing with Him, asking Him to guide and direct our life, and trying, as best we can, to be faithful disciples. He offers His help to all of us who want to find the true meaning of life and "save" our life in the right way. We lose by saving, and save by losing! It's that simple.

We Can Change

Genesis 9:8-17 and Mark 1:9-15

"Wherefore . . . I was not disobedient to the heavenly vision, but declared . . . that they should repent and turn to God and perform deeds worthy of their repentance." ACTS 26:19, 20B (RSV)

IN ALL OF US, I SUSPECT, THERE ARE ATTITUDES lurking that need to change. It may be a short temper, ready to flare up and hurt those we love. It may be some hurt or bitterness we have harbored secretly for years. It may be resentment that we can no longer do the things we always did. Especially as we grow older, we may be surprised and dismayed that our bodies are so vulnerable to pain. A friend of mine is facing a serious, very serious problem that involves increasing weakness in his body. He is having to cope, not only with the physical weakness, but with his emotional reactions to it. So his "repentance" involves giving up self-pity and choosing to believe the good news that God is in charge and will not abandon him!

Repentance means turning to a new direction. If we have been fearful, it means turning against our fear and choosing to trust. If we have been grouchy, it means turning against our demanding self-love, and choosing to be cheerful. And so on.

We may know we have some negative attitudes, but choose to think, "Well, that's the way it is. I wish I were otherwise but that's the way I am."

Jesus, on the other hand, is saying, "There is hope. You can change. Believe the good news. God's kingdom is at hand." And in another place He reminds us, "The kingdom is within you." (Luke 17:21)

Prayer

Eternal God, our heavenly Father: take from us all wrong thoughts and affections, all selfish and unworthy desires. Enable us to hate everything that is evil in Your sight and to love what You love. We ask this through Jesus Christ our Lord. Amen.

A Step Further

*Then he called the crowd
to him along with his
disciples and said: "If anyone
would come after me, he
must deny himself and
take up his cross and
follow me."*

MARK 8:34 (NIV)

Retirement

Retirement! The word didn't sound like something my husband would ever want to do. But suddenly, he was sixty years old and making his decision to "get out while he was still ahead and in his right mind."

His responsibilities as chairman of one of the then "Big Eight" accounting firms were a constant pressure. Even though he was good at what he did, he had been losing weight, pushing food around on his plate, and looking off into space a lot recently. Was it the pressure of the job, or the thought of quitting what he had always loved to do? Either way, there was no looking back! His mind was made up.

I was certainly having second thoughts. I would miss the company of some really wonderful friends—both the men and their wives who made up the inner circle of his company. I would miss the traveling that had become part of our routine. Unfortunately, the anxiety and sense of loss didn't cause me to push the food around on my plate—it all went in my mouth where it had always gone.

Several months before the dreaded final day in September when Bill would pack up his belongings and move out of the corner office, the firm held a seminar for all retiring partners and their wives. At the first session, a psychologist asked each of us to think of one word to describe our reaction to "retirement." She then went around the room, hearing the answers. "Leisure," "golf," "travel," "Florida"—well, you get the picture—everyone was definitely looking forward to this time of life. I broke out in a cold sweat! There was only one word that had occurred to me. Oh help! I couldn't think of anything else. Finally, it was Bill's turn and he said "Fun." Trembling, not trusting my own voice, I blurted out, "Fear!"

The psychologist had several couples who had retired the year before tell their story, and most of what they said was a lesson in what *not* to do.

—"Don't sell your house and move right away." Good, we'd already done that and didn't plan to move again.

—"Don't plan on spending every waking moment together; make sure he knows you married him for better or worse but not for lunch." Don't worry! We have spent well over half of our married life separated by continents and oceans, so I couldn't see us suddenly sitting in each other's laps all day.

—"Each partner should develop some interests of their own; don't count on your children to keep you entertained." We had plenty of interests already, and our children all had lives of their own and were fully as independent as we were. My fears quieted some.

The retirement party in September, swansong to a career of thirty-eight years, was a lovely refined affair, but suddenly it was all over, and we were the owners of a beautiful Steuben world globe. That was ten years ago.

In Roget's *International Thesaurus*, other words for retirement are retreat, recession, disemployment, reticence, privacy, resignation and seclusion. So I guess you could say that neither of us has really gone into retirement, as none of those words seem to apply.

I went to work four years ago at one of those half-time jobs that is really full-time and then some. Bill still has an office in New York. He is on several boards and still travels around the world. And I still go with him. We have enjoyed working together on fund-raising and traveling with our church's internationally acclaimed choir. On each of our tours, we received more than we were able to give.

All in all getting older is not bad—just keep your sense of humor, because some days the spirit is willing but the flesh is weak. Advice? Yep! Get up and do something for someone else—even if it's just giving them a smile. You'll be glad you did.

Sally Kanaga

The Cost of Obedience FEBRUARY 1

Psalm 104:1-24A and Hebrews 5:1-10

*Although he was a son, yet he learned obedience
from what He suffered.* HEBREWS 5:8 (NIV)

THIS IS ONE OF THE STRANGEST VERSES IN THE BIBLE. It brings us face to face with the great "stooping down" of God in the Incarnation. As Christians we believe that Jesus is not just a man, not even the best man who ever lived. He is that, and more. We believe that He is God Incarnate, the Word made flesh who dwelt among us. He is the Second Person of the Holy Trinity. And that is what makes this verse from the Letter to the Hebrews so remarkable. Here we have not some play-acting divinity who pretends to be human, but a man like us, Jesus our brother, who *learns* from His earthly experiences and is changed by them. This insight into His earthly life brings Him nearer to us in our experiences, since it shows He understands, because He has "been there."

These words are written to people who have made a decision to obey God. We too may have made this decision in many past instances, and at times may not even be aware of it. But from all of us, sooner or later, He asks what we find most costly. He asks us to obey when it hurts, when our will and His will are very far apart. What do we do then? Do we say, "This is too high a price! I can't do that! I won't do that!"

Whatever it may be that God is calling us to accept as an act of obedience, we know that it will not be as costly as the price our Lord paid. In carrying out His life of obedience to His Father's will, He paid a price we can only faintly imagine. I believe He is ready to teach us from His own experience, and that He stands with us as we bear whatever cross He asks of us.

Having given us His best in becoming our Savior, He knows that we will never be satisfied if we hold back our best. And our best may be just the willingness to bear some hard obedience, some difficult situation or condition He asks of us.

Standing on the Promises of God   February 2

Genesis 15:1-12, 17-18 and Philippians 3:17-4:1

*Therefore, my brethren, whom I love and long for, my joy and
crown, stand firm thus in the Lord, my beloved.*
Philippians 4:1 (rsv)

"You can depend on it" is a theme used by countless
advertisers to sell their product. They know that everyone
is looking for something that is dependable, and never breaks
down. The only problem is that such a product of human
hands has never existed. In fact, it seems that the more we
count on something to perform in a pinch, the more likely it
will fail us.

People can let us down. We expect someone to come
through for us, only to be disappointed and hurt when they do
not deliver. And there have been times when we, too, have broken a promise, or hurt someone else's feelings. Neither things or
people are always dependable.

I recall a time when I had promised to visit an elderly
woman who lived alone. A day late, I suddenly remembered
that I was to have called on her the afternoon before. I called
her, only to find that she had waited for me, with refreshments
prepared and ready, but I had never arrived. She was understanding and generous in her forgiveness. Neither things nor
people are always dependable, and if we are honest with ourselves, we will admit that it is sadly true of us as well.

Then who can we rely on? Is there something or someone
who will never disappoint us, who will never break down at the
most crucial of times? The Bible answers the question with a
resounding, "Yes." "Jesus Christ is the same yesterday, today
and forever," says the writer to the Hebrews (13:8). "For no
matter how many promises God has made, they are 'Yes' in
Christ" (II Cor. 1:20, niv)

A look at the life of Abraham is one illustration of this
wonderful truth. To Abraham was given the promise that he

would become the father of a multitude, and that all nations would be blessed through him. Now, thousands of years later, we who bear the name of Christian are a part of Gods fulfilling what seems to be an impossible promise.

Like solid rock, the promises of God can bear the weight of all our hopes and expectations. As the Scriptures say, "Whoever believes in him will never be disappointed" (Isaiah 28:16; Romans 10:11). And, thanks be to God, the Bible has never been guilty of false advertising.

Leaving All for Him   February 3

Jonah 3 and Mark 1:14-20

"He called them; and they left their father Zebedee in the boat with the hired men, and followed him."   Mark 1:20 (NIV)

BOTH OF THE SCRIPTURE LESSONS FOR TODAY have to do with leaving something behind to grasp what lies ahead. The people of Ninevah were preached to by that strange-looking prophet Jonah, who must have been pretty well bleached-out after his sojourn in the "belly of the fish." His message was so stark and startling that he didn't even bother telling them what they needed to forsake. He simply announced that the city would be destroyed in forty days. But they knew God well enough to believe, even in the face of such an absolute pronouncement, that "His mercies are over all His works." *And* they knew very well what they needed to leave behind: their sinful, selfish, disobedient ways. And so they repented, and prayed for mercy—and it came.

Jesus' message in Mark Chapter One is a very simple one: "The kingdom of God is at hand: Repent and believe in the gospel [the Good News]." Then he began to call disciples to follow Him, promising to make those fishermen by the Galilean Lake, "fishers of men." They would go out with their message and "catch" people for the Kingdom of God!

In today's lesson—Simon (later named Peter) and Andrew, ". . . immediately left their nets . . ." Have you ever thought about the breath-taking dimension of that? Their nets were their livelihood. Fishing was the only occupation they knew. Their families depended on them for support. But here was a call that was so strong, so intense, so ennobling, so full of hope and purpose that they could not refuse it. "Immediately" says it quite well. No hesitation, arguing, asking for easier terms. They just left and followed.

No one follows Jesus without leaving something behind. It may be old sins. It may be undue attachment to father or mother, wife or husband, son or daughter. It may be a life of busyness, doing a work that we thought gave our life its meaning. It may be old griefs, bad memories (or good ones), or any number of other "things" that He asks us to let go of and leave behind. Like the broken nets of the Galilean fishermen, we *can* choose to leave the past behind and live in the present moment. We do not have to peer into the future and wonder and worry about what it will hold. Whatever it holds, we will not be asked to face it alone. His presence will lighten every darkness and lift every burden.

The Name that is Above Every Name   FEBRUARY 4

Philippians 2:5-11 and Matthew 21:1-11

He humbled Himself and became obedient unto death, even death on a cross. Therefore God has highly exalted Him and bestowed on Him the name which is above every name. . . .
PHIL. 2:8B, 9 (RSV)

BEHOLD, YOUR KING IS COMING TO YOU, *humble and mounted on an ass, and on a colt, the foal of an ass. (Matt. 21:5)*
As the crowds waved branches to welcome the King, Jesus

rode, not to a throne but to a Cross. Ahead there lay not a royal diadem but a crown of thorns.

The only triumph awaiting Jesus was the triumph of God's purpose in and through Him—the triumph of love over hatred, of mercy over malice, of obedience over rebellion.

The path to glory for Jesus was that of humiliation, degradation, and death. He gave up all that was dear to Him—save only His love for God and His obedience to the Father. He let go all earthly ties—even His dear Mother.

Is it a surprise that He calls us to walk the same path that He walked? Is it strange that we, too, must lay aside our claims on everything that ties us to this earth, so that God might be our all in all? If we believe in Him, if we love Him, if we desire to be like Him and to be with Him, He has a simple word for us: "He who loses his life for my sake shall find it." That word is sealed with His own life's Blood.

Day by day, we are given a chance to honor His name. Most of us will show that love and reverence by the attitudes we take towards our life, the circumstances we cannot change, the people we live with, the things we must do or the things we cannot do. If in our hearts we choose to let our circumstances whittle away our self-love and self-concern, then we are loving and honoring Jesus. If we choose to become rigid and bitter, feeling that we are victims of unfairness, then we are turning our backs on His love, His sacrifice, and His cross. He seeks to bring us what the world cannot give—peace that passes understanding, forgiveness for all that is past, and hope for all that is to come. Blessed be His Name!

Prayers and Promises   FEBRUARY 5

II Peter 3:1-10 and Matthew 28:16-20

The Lord is not slack concerning His promise.   II PETER 3:9 (KJV)

MANY OF US WONDER WHY GOD DOES NOT act sooner. The psalmist asks, "O Lord God of hosts, how long wilt Thou be angry with Thy people's prayers?" The prophet laments, "O Lord, how long shall I cry and Thou wilt not hear?" (Hab. 1:2)

Writing to persecuted Christians, Peter realizes that they are in danger of giving in to despair and hopelessness. Scoffers were asking, "Where is the promise of His coming?"

Has it not been the same with us when we have long prayed for something that seemed good and right, but was not forthcoming? Doubts and accusations arise. The accuser whispers, "It's no use! God doesn't hear—or care!"

What should we do then? Peter's answer is simple: Do not draw back! Press harder! Look farther! We are dealing with the God of the Ages. We are conversing with the One who inhabits eternity and sees far beyond the limited scope of our vision.

A group of clergy, concerned about making their message relevant in a changing world, asked a well-known minister, "How can you preach the Gospel in a world that might be blown up by an atomic bomb any day?" His answer: "The time frame of this earthly life is not the limit of the Gospel."

Corrie Ten Boom, who lived to tell how God had sustained her through the horrors of a Nazi concentration camp, used to say, "Heaven has no panic; only plans."

So, when the answer to our prayers is delayed, it is all part of a greater plan. Peter says the delay in Jesus' coming is linked to His unwillingness "that any should perish." The door is still ajar. The welcome mat is still out. The Spirit still moves in rebellious hearts to convince them of their need of a Savior. Such is God's delaying mercy.

And all those unfulfilled promises we depend on? What in us needs to surrender our will to His? What in us needs the purifying and purging effect of unanswered prayer? Let our sight come into clearer focus, so our prayer will not be a demand but an instrument by which His will comes about—in ourselves and in others. Let faith grow in its insistent need, until the promise is fulfilled, because "the Lord is not slack concerning His promise."

Praying for Others   FEBRUARY 6

Psalm 14 and Ephesians 3:14-21

[I pray] that according to the riches of His glory, He may grant that you be strengthened with might through His Spirit, . . . and that Christ may dwell in your hearts through faith; that you . . . may have power . . . to know the love of Christ which surpasses knowledge. EPHESIANS 3:16-19 (RSV) (SELECTIONS)

IT MAY BE THE MOST IMPORTANT THING YOU CAN DO. Praying for others, that is. I was very struck by the words of a nineteenth-century physician who combined prayer with medical remedies in his New York sanitarium. Here is one thing he said about prayer:

"According to God's plan of governing He has set prayer, the prayer of faith, as the one force by which He governs the world. Stronger than gravitation, than light or heat, exalted above all. He has set prayer to lay hold upon and control all other forces and move them, to bring honor to Himself. That is why He is asking us to pray without ceasing, and in everything to give thanks."

The thing that struck me in those words was the bold assertion that prayer is "the one force" by which God governs the world. What a thought! We know that Jesus told us to pray and said that if our faith was as a mustard seed, we could move mountains. And we have heard many testimonies of how prayer changed situations or changed people. It seems to me that praying for others is simply accepting the invitation of the Lord to join with Him in blessing them. He wants to bless and He is willing to allow us to have a part in that blessing if we pray faithfully.

Hymn

> Before our Father's throne
> We pour our ardent prayers;
> Our fears, our hopes, our aims are one,
> Our comforts and our cares.

Prayer Makes a Difference   FEBRUARY 7

Psalm 14 and Ephesians 3:14-21

The prayer of a righteous man has great power in its effects.
JAMES 5:16B (RSV)

THE QUESTION THEN IS, WHY DON'T WE TAKE PRAYER more seriously, and really hold up those we love to the Lord for His blessing.

When Augustine's mother saw him living in sin and knew that his life was one of waste and destruction, she kept praying for him. Year after year she held him before the Lord and pleaded for his salvation. When she spoke to her bishop, St Ambrose, he assured her that "the child of so many tears could not be lost." She lived to see Augustine become a Christian, and felt that her life-work was accomplished. She did not, of course, know that 1500 years later we would still be reading his writings and would call him "St Augustine."

Are we praying for those we love, believing that somehow God will incorporate our feeble, weak prayers into His mighty mercy system—and that our prayers make a difference? I hope so! What an exciting possibility it is, even if we are limited in our activity by age or by infirmity, to see that prayer reaches beyond the physical locality—and *does* make a difference.

Many people I know have a monthly prayer list. Knowing

how hard it is always to remember everyone who should be remembered, they keep a little list to remind them for whom to pray. Their prayers may be very simple, even childlike. But we can never, never calculate the good that can come from them.

A dear friend sent me these words recently: "Sick, suffering, and sorrowing people cannot see their fellow believers who are praying for them. But many people have told me they are amazed at the sense of God's presence in their affliction, and they know this to be the result of the prayers of their friends." (Anon.)

The Puzzle of Unanswered Prayer   FEBRUARY 8

I Kings 3:5-12 and Romans 8: 26-34

We do not know how to pray as we ought, but the Spirit Himself intercedes for us with sighs too deep for words.
ROMANS 8:26B (RSV)

PRAYER HAS ALWAYS BEEN A MYSTERY for people of faith. We who believe that we have a Heavenly Father, a Savior, and an indwelling Presence, the Holy Spirit, sometimes find ourselves wondering about prayer.

In my younger days, I remember seeing a motto used as an illuminated decoration on the walls of homes. It read: "Prayer changes things. Pray without ceasing." Now that I'm older I know that the motto is indeed true: Prayer changes things. It would be impossible to enumerate the number of situations that have "changed" when we prayed about them. So, I know that Jesus was serious when He told us that we should ask what we will in His name, and He would give it.

I also have known times when prayers seemed unanswered. Crying out in need and desperation in an impossible situation, I have felt that I did not receive an answer. The situation did not get better. This has been the experience of millions as they faced the evils of war or personal tragedy.

Yet Paul says here, "The Spirit Himself intercedes for us with sighs too deep for words." Somehow in that mystery of prayer, God Himself enters. The situation about which we are praying cannot be altered. Yet prayer changes things. Prayer unites us with God. The Spirit enters our pain, our fear, our worry. He cares. He groans for us and in us. What a picture of God's infinite love! One of the saints said, "Prayer oneth the soul with God."

The hymn writer boldly prays, "Teach me the patience of unanswered prayer." Even unanswered prayer changes things. It clears away the cobwebs of selfish desire. It helps us become humble, submissive before the Creator. It "ones" our souls with Divine purposes. And that is not something to be dismissed lightly. Prayer remains a mystery. But how bright a mystery it is, burning with eternal truths and eternal hopes.

Jesus' Prayer For Us FEBRUARY 9

I John 5:9-13 and John 17:11B-19

Holy Father, keep them in Thy name which thou hast given me . . . I pray not for these only, but also for those who are to believe in me through their word. JOHN 17:11B, 20 (RSV)

DO YOU EVER THINK ABOUT THE FACT THAT JESUS Himself prayed for you? Here, as He faced His final agony in His earthly life, His concern was focused on those for whom He came: those who had been His followers and companions during His earthly ministry, and those who would come after them. That includes you and me.

It is not surprising that this would be the case. If we love someone, we are concerned about his welfare. And since Jesus' life was a life of unlimited, self-giving love, it is not surprising that He would be concerned for those who had loved Him and believed in Him.

When we forget that He prays for us, we may mistakenly think that we are having to face life alone. I have been reading lately a book in which a doctor interviews people who are very sick. One thing that impresses me is that these people tell again and again how important their faith is in getting through their difficulties. They say things like, "I don't know how I could make it without my faith." Another thing, however, that also impresses me is that when people are very sick, they confess that at times they feel alone—especially in the long night hours, when there is no one to talk to.

If you ever have times like these, I would suggest that it is a very good time to remind yourself that Jesus cares, that He is very near, and that you can call out to Him, even in your silent prayers. Other people are important to us, but there comes a time in all our lives when we must "walk the lonesome valley." But we do not walk alone, even when we *feel* alone. The psalmist said it so well: "I will fear no evil, for *Thou* art with me."

I am grateful for those who pray for me, and I am grateful that I have the privilege of praying for others. And I am even more grateful for being included in our Lord's "High Priestly Prayer." For I know that the Father hears and is well pleased with that prayer.

And He Prayed   FEBRUARY 10

Job 7:1-7 and Mark 1:29-39

And in the morning, a great while before day, He rose and went out to a lonely place, and there He prayed.   MARK 1:35 (RSV)

JOB'S WORDS IN TODAY'S OLD TESTAMENT lesson are filled with bitterness and despair. He keeps arguing with God and with his friends that he is right and righteous, and does not deserve all the calamities that have befallen him. We can understand how he felt for our prayers, too, have been full of complaint. There are many things in life to make us angry—*if* we choose to get angry about them. Somehow our prayer must move beyond these selfish, accusing thoughts that imply that God is not good.

In today's Gospel, Jesus is still near the beginning of His ministry—a ministry which He knew would lead Him to the cross. He would not be a success in the eyes of the world. It would seem that His enemies would win over Him. But Jesus kept Himself armed with the same weapons we have: constant faithful prayer. He stayed in communion with His heavenly Father. "A great while before day" He went out to arm Himself with spiritual strength. Then He was ready to get on with His life.

We have the same resources that Jesus had: the Holy Spirit of God. In prayer we connect our lives anew with Him and His purposes. We offer our thanks and praise for what is past. We renew our faith, hope, and trust for all that is to come. In Jesus' words, we may pray, "Give us today our daily bread." That is, sufficient strength for today. Surely if He, the Son of God, felt the need to pray, how much more should we count it not only a privilege but an urgent necessity.

With prayer, we can face any difficulty and not be overwhelmed by it. If we are followers of Jesus, we must learn to pray. And the only way to learn is by doing it.

Established Hearts   FEBRUARY 11

Isaiah 35:1-10 and James 5:7-10

Behold, the farmer waits for the precious fruit of the earth, being
patient over it until it receives the early and the late rain. You
also be patient. Establish your hearts, for the coming
of the Lord is at hand.   JAMES 5:7B, 8 (RSV)

IT IS SOMETHING OF A MYSTERY TO ALL OF US—how some
prayers get answered immediately, while others seem be to
delayed interminably.

I could name at least half a dozen "prayer concerns" that I
have been praying for a long time that still haven't been
answered *as far as I can see.* These have to do with people I love
and my concern for their eternal welfare. So, what do we do in
such a case? Give up praying and decide (as the Devil would
like us to) that praying does no good? I, for one, am not willing to do that! So I keep going back to the throne of grace and
make my request to my heavenly Father. It is not mine to say
when or how these prayers will be answered. It is rather mine
to continue to believe and let the delay do its work in me.

The older I get the more I realize how "unestablished" my
heart is in the face of tragedy or crisis. It seems to take only a
little thing to upset my tranquility, and then it takes some doing
to get it back again. But thanks be to God, the process is not
finished! The encouraging thing is that all these delays, all the
great promises that have been given to us, and all the evidence
we have of answered prayer in the past, combine to "establish
our hearts."

James puts it in the context of the imminent coming of the
Lord. We know that other generations expected that the
Kingdom would come in its fullness in their lifetimes, and that the
expected end did not come. But that does not negate the truth
in this verse. For the "coming of the Lord" is not just at the end
of history or the end of this age. It is also His coming to answer

our need. Silently, almost secretly, He arrives in the midst of our need and speaks peace to our hearts. That is His way, and we can be assured that He will never fail to arrive on time.

On Being Content   FEBRUARY 12

Hebrews 13:1-8 AND Luke 14:1-14

. . . And be content with what you have; for He has said,
"I will never fail you nor forsake you."   HEB. 13:5 (RSV)

WE LIVE IN A WORLD OF DISCONTENT. It seems discontentment is everywhere. Wars, riots, crime, drugs—all are expressions of intense discontent in people's hearts. Each of us faces discontentment at some level. The world knows this and plays to our inner discontent, offering us all kinds of remedies via advertising and commercials.

Our text says simply, "Be content with what you have, for the Lord has said, 'I will never fail you nor forsake you.'" Our contentment *must* move from looking at outward things to having something within that gives us peace. I recently talked with a dear lady who was distressed and in tears because of things in her family that she could not change. As we talked, it seemed important to focus, not on the things that were distressing her, but on her inner attitude of *allowing* these things to bother her so much. So, at her request, we prayed together that she be able to relinquish these situations to the Lord, and choose to believe that He is in each one of them, working for good. That is such an important point that I cannot stress it too much.

It is not enough just to pray for a certain situation. If we want to have our wills in harmony with the will of God, we must make choices, and do the hard work of letting go our demand that things be the way we would like to have them. God knows best. He is already at work in every situation and He has a plan that is larger than we can imagine. He sees down the road, whereas we can only see the here and now. He works for good. He works in love. He works in mercy. We can let go our demand and say to Him, "Father, I do not understand You, but I trust You. I give You permission to do what You know best, and I thank You for the grace to let go."

Being content is a way of showing our faith, of demonstrating before the visible and invisible world that we love God and that we trust His infinite goodness.

But What are They Among So Many?   FEBRUARY 13

Joshua 1:1-9 and Job 6:5-14

There is a lad here who has five barley loaves and two fish;
but what are they among so many?   JOHN 6:9 (RSV)

TODAY'S GOSPEL LESSON IS ONE OF THE MOST familiar stories in the New Testament. The Gospel writers enjoy retelling this demonstration of Jesus' miraculous power. It never grows old.

First, the story says that God is able to supply our needs, no matter what the "odds" may be. Too many of us underrate God. We underestimate His power in the specific situation we may be facing. This story says there are no impossibilities with God. That does not give us *carte blanche* to presume on Him. Whatever He does, He must be consistent with Himself and His own divine will. But aside from that—what limits are there? Only our faith. He, the Almighty God, *permits* Himself to be limited by our puny faith!

Second, the story says that God uses the most unlikely instruments in accomplishing His purpose. The little lad with his lunch had the privilege of giving over to others what may have seemed too much for him. Once he had done that, what a thrill it must have been for him to see what Jesus did with his gift. God does ask us to "let goods and kindred go, this mortal life also," in the sense of trying to save them for themselves. But

once we have given them over to Him, no matter how insignificant our gifts may seem, God uses them to bless others.

You may feel you have little to contribute to others any
more. Your life may have become constrained, restricted—how
can you make much difference in the world? But small though
your circle of influence may be, it is important to God. The little
boy may not have known who was receiving his lunch. But
Jesus received it and used it. And He will receive our gift—even
if it is only the *willingness* to be where we are without murmuring or complaining! To do that can be a great offering of
ourselves to God. So think about what you can offer Him in
your present circumstance: prayers, thanksgivings, a cheerful
countenance, loving concern for others. These are not small
gifts, and God will bless them if we offer them in love to Him.

With All Your Heart FEBRUARY 14

Deuteronomy 6:1-9 and Mark 12:28-34

*Hear O Israel: The Lord our God, is one Lord; and you shall
love the Lord your God with all your heart, and with all your
soul and with all your might.* DEUT. 6:4-5 (RSV)

THIS WAS ONE OF THE MOST IMPORTANT VERSES in Scriptures
for the people of Israel. It sums up the very nature of their
faith and what God expected from them as His people. He, the
Lord, is one, not many gods. At the center of the universe, at
the core of life there is one Presence.

Israel's God, who had revealed Himself to Abraham, Isaac,
and Jacob and who had given them the Law under Moses, was
holy, consistent, true, almighty, and all merciful. Over and over,
the prophets called the people back to live lives that would be
consistent with the nature of the God they worshipped.

Jesus underscored the importance of this verse when He
quoted it as a summation of the whole Law in these words: love

the Lord with all your heart, soul, and might. If the heart, soul, and might are centered on God, all the right things will fall into place. Jesus, of course, added the "second commandment" saying we should love our neighbor as ourselves.

Why did God speak to us in this way? (For this is a word to all of us, of whatever generation, race or nation, if we would be part of God's People.) Why does He ask us to love Him with all our heart, soul, and might? Because in loving Him we find life, and we leave behind the dregs and bitter fruit of our fallen nature. In loving Him we enter into a life of hope and "peace with God which passes all understanding."

We do not make God richer by loving Him. But we are enriched beyond words. Paul says that Jesus became poor that we through His poverty might enjoy the riches of God. That's why God asks us to love Him; that we might enjoy His riches. And He never asks us to do anything without giving us the grace to do it.

The Peril of Stubborn Unbelief   FEBRUARY 15

I Timothy 6:6-19 and Luke 16:19-31

"Neither will they be convinced if someone should rise from the dead."   LUKE 16:31B (RSV)

JESUS' STORY OF THE RICH MAN AND LAZARUS was aimed at people who stubbornly refused to believe. They saw the miracles He did, they heard His gracious words, but they did not *choose* to believe in Him. In another place, John's Gospel says, "This is the condemnation: that light has come into the world and that men prefer darkness to light, because their deeds are evil." The condemnation is that light is refused.

I suppose we have all been guilty of stubborn unbelief. I remember my sister saying, "I'm seeing it but I'm not believing it." She would not change her mind on a certain subject even when her eyes told her she was wrong!

Why do we choose not to believe the Truth? Is it because the truth will require that we do something we don't like doing? Maybe it will mean that we have to forgive someone against whom we have (we think) a justifiable grudge. I know that's hard for me at times! Maybe the truth will require that we stop complaining about some situation we don't like.

Jesus is talking about people who just would not acknowledge Him as the Messiah, as the Anointed one sent from God to save them. And so they "missed the boat." How sad! God loved them and it was His will that they find life. Jesus said, "I came that they might have life and have it more abundantly.

I have always been leery of believing too much. I have been afraid of being deluded or duped. Not believing had a certain appeal, because it meant I wasn't going to "play the fool and fall for everything." I know, however, that I have forfeited peace and blessing by being too stubborn. I pray now that I may be more childlike, more open to the wonder of the spirit, less afraid to believe. After all, Jesus said that unless we turn and become "as little children" we will miss the kingdom of heaven.

Stop, Look, and Listen   FEBRUARY 16

I Samuel 3:1-10 and John 1:35-42

Go lie down, and if He calls you, you shall say, "Speak Lord, for Thy servant hears."   I SAM. 3:9 (RSV)

THE SCRIPTURES TODAY ARE CALLING US TO STOP, look, and listen. The boy Samuel was told, in the words of our text, to respond to the voice he was hearing. John tells those who are coming to be baptized by him, "Look! the Lamb of God!" And when two of the disciples went to Jesus to ask where He lived, they were told "Come and see." Over and over Scriptures tell us that there is something to *hear* if we have ears to hear, and that there is something to *see* if we will stop and look.

Did you ever think of how many voices clamor for your ears each day? Since the invention of the radio and television, many of us spend many hours daily having our ears bombarded with trivia, sales pitches, and even more sinister sounds. The cumulative effect is to dull our hearing—and our conscience.

I attended a retreat recently in which we were given large blocks of time to be quiet. One person said, "I was actually *afraid* to face that silence." I heard a well-known personality on TV recently say, "Solitude is creative; isolation is dangerous." Whether we have little amounts of silence or larger ones, the question is, how do we make use of it?

Many people have "time on their hands." This may seem a terrible burden. It often encourages loneliness or self-pity, because we cannot change the outward circumstance. The solution to the problem and the way to avoid these deadly emotions is to claim the quietness for worthwhile purposes, for a more meaningful communion with our Heavenly Father. Even when we cannot read long hours, we can still contemplate the goodness and mercy of the Lord. We can focus our minds on Jesus and His love for us, even if for only short periods at a time.

We must take time to listen for the quiet Voice within. We must choose to listen with our hearts. It is important that we, like young Samuel, can say, "Speak, Lord, for Thy servant heareth."

Our Need is to Be Small   FEBRUARY 17

Ephesians 2:11-18 and Mark 6:30-34

And Jesus said to them, "Come away by yourselves to a lonely place and rest a while." MARK 6:31 (RSV)

THE THEME OF TODAY IS "REST": our need of it and God's provision for it.

Jesus said, "Come away by yourselves to a lonely place and rest a while." These moments when we draw aside to worship and pray can be rest for our spirits—a refreshing and renewing rest. We can lay down the burdens which we have dragged along with us. Here, before the mighty throne of God, we may cast them aside and let them go. The burden of sin and guilt: forgiveness is here. The burden of fear: peace and hope are here. The burden of resentments and bitterness: reconciling grace is here. The burden of fretfulness and sadness: joy is here.

And in addition to these quiet times of meditation and worship, we can all make room for God's peace. It will take some determination on our part. It will mean turning off the TV, laying aside the newspaper or magazines, getting over our fear that others might think we are a little peculiar! But there is peace, there is holy rest to be found—from the Prince of Peace, the giver of peace.

Harry Emerson Fosdick said, "Our need is to be still." He was pastor of one of New York City's great churches. There he rubbed shoulders with the captains of industry and finance. He knew the struggle and clamor of the world. And at one time, it became too much for him. He had to lay everything aside and go for healing—inner healing of the soul and emotions. But what he learned in that time of brokenness never failed him. He remembered, "Our need is to be still."

Are you in a time when God has set you aside from the activity you have known in other years? Let it be a time to "come apart and rest." Let it be a time to savor the peace of His eternity. It is His loving gift. "Teach us, beyond our striving, the rich rewards of rest."

Find Rest For Your Souls   FEBRUARY 18

Psalm 65 and Matthew 11:25-30

*Come to me, all you who labor and are heavy-laden, and I will
give you rest. Take my yoke upon you and learn from me;
for I am gentle and lowly in heart, and you will find rest
for your souls.* MATT. 11:28, 29 (RSV)

A FRIEND OF OURS RECENTLY said that she had always had a
dissatisfied, unfulfilled inner life.

In truth, much of my inner life, too, has been marked by a
sense of unfulfillment and lack of peace. When my older sister
died earlier this year, I was confronted anew with the fact that
we have no long-term claim on life. We either find the peace
and rest which Jesus talks about now, or go on in dissatisfaction and, possibly, adding to our bitterness and frustration.

Jesus knows how harried and worried we often are. That is
why He talked so much about not worrying about the future,
about learning from the birds to trust our Heavenly Father's
care, about what we can learn from the lilies of the field. He
says that we are of great value to God because God has chosen
to love us. If we allow that truth to become a reality in our
lives, much of our fretting and worrying will dissipate. What
the future holds is under His control. He will not leave us to
face it alone, and He will give us grace, day by day, to meet
what it brings.

There are times in our lives when we have to lay aside much
of our work and activity—temporarily or more permanently.
Time weighs heavily on your hands, because you have been
used to *doing*, amounting to something, contributing your
share. And now you may feel very frustrated because those
avenues of self-expression seem closed to you.

But wait! There are others still open. You can still pray. You
can still add cheer rather than gloom to your surroundings.
Above all, you can *learn* from Jesus this secret of rest. Earlier in

your life you may have been too busy to think much about this. Now, He invites you to come aside with Him, to grow inwardly more like the person you always wanted to be. He is there to help you, to encourage you, to "find rest for your soul."

He is Able   FEBRUARY 19

Mark 10:13-16 and Hebrews 2:9-18

For because He Himself has suffered and been tempted, He is able to help those who are tempted. HEBREWS 2:18 (RSV)

WE'VE ALL KNOW PEOPLE WHO SEEMED to have such a high opinion of themselves that they were ready to condemn out of hand anyone who fell into sin or did wrong of any kind.

The New Testament gives us an entirely different picture of Jesus. A woman caught in the act of adultery, who was going to be stoned to death, was "rescued" by Jesus with these words- "He who is without sin among you, let him cast the first stone." They were so convicted that they left one by one. When they all had gone, Jesus asked the woman, "Where are your accusers? Has no one condemned you?" And she answered, "No one, Lord." He said, "Neither do I condemn you. Go and do not sin again."

We know that Jesus did not make light of sin. We know that He died on the cross that we might be forgiven and set free from our sins. But that is not all. He has "suffered and been tempted." In another place we are told, "He was tempted in all points as we are, yet without sinning." So He understands us better than we do ourselves!

Sometimes people come to a minister with a tale of shame they have carried for years. It is a burden on their heart, and it makes them afraid. They think that they have to go through life and into the next carrying the burden. But remember John Bunyan's Christian in *Pilgrim's Progress*. When he looked at the cross, his burden was loosed off his back, rolled down the hill into a sepulchre, and was seen no more. That represents what Jesus Christ does with our shame and sin when we confess to Him and ask forgiveness.

As I read the words of today's text, I think of a chorus I've heard many times,

He is able, he is able, I know He is able

I know my Lord is able to carry us through.

And that is what I would like to leave with you today. Our God is able. Our Savior, Jesus Christ, knows and understands you just where you are. He knows your struggles, failures, shame, guilt, and fear. Do not hesitate to call on Him for help, for forgiveness, for release from anxiety. He is able.

He Came For Us   FEBRUARY 20

Genesis 22:1-18 and Matthew 9:9-13

I came not to call the righteous, but sinners. MATTHEW 9:13 (RSV)

WHO ARE THESE "SINNERS" JESUS CAME TO CALL? Are they not those who acknowledge their wrongness? People who are right trust in their own goodness to make them right with God. The Bible warns us that such trust is misplaced. Before God "there is none righteous, no, not one." Before God, who is pure and holy, our righteousness is as "filthy rags."

But Jesus sought out those who were considered unworthy. He ate with tax collectors and sinners. Some time ago I read this headline in a Christian publication: *Prison Bars Keep These Cons In But Can't Keep the Power Of God Out*

The article told of men who had found God behind prison bars. "God brought me to prison to set me free," said one. "I'd rather be right here with Jesus Christ than anywhere else in the world without Him."

There are different kinds of prisons. There are prisons with bars. And there are those in which we find ourselves—such as nursing homes or hospitals—where we cannot do what we want when we want. Will this be a time of knowing Jesus—or will we become bitter and resentful?

The way to find God's peace and joy is to face our wrongness. We must let God show us where our attitudes and actions have not been what they should have been. Perhaps we were self-centered, demanding our own way, ill-tempered, insisting that people love us instead of seeking to love them. When we take our wrongness to Him, not making excuses for it, He forgives us and gives us His righteousness. What an exchange! Our wrongness for His righteousness, our guilt for His forgiveness, our sadness for His joy!

Jesus loves us. He invites us to love Him with all our heart, soul, mind, and strength. And He invites us to love our neighbor as much as we have loved ourselves. In doing that, we will begin to know a peace "that passes all understanding," and a joy that no one and no circumstance can take away.

A wise once person said, "It's not our sin that keeps us from Jesus. It's our goodness." Our rightness can keep us from the peace of knowing our sins are forgiven. What a poor choice if we choose rightness instead of Jesus!

The Story of the Two Sons   FEBRUARY 21

Luke 15:11-32

And [his father] said to him, "Son you are always with me,
and all that is mine is yours."   LUKE 15:31 (RSV)

WE CALL THIS THE PARABLE OF THE PRODIGAL SON, because it is one of the most tender and wonderful stories ever told—about a wayward, rebellious young man who was allowed to come to the end of himself, and who woke up in time to realize his mistake and return to his father.

What a picture that is! It recalls the words of one of the greatest of all the hymns we sing:" "Amazing grace! how sweet the sound, that saved a wretch like me! I once was lost, but now am found! Was blind, but now I see." Who has not felt the joy of heart this story brings, just in telling it or reading it over. And this is especially true if you are one of those who wandered into a "far country" and found that all the joy of it turned sour and bitter, and that you were starving for what you could find only at your Father's house. St Augustine says, "Our hearts are restless, until we find our rest in Thee." And that is true—wonderfully true!

There is another thing about this story that gladdens our hearts. It is the picture our Lord painted of our heavenly Father waiting for us to wake up and come back home. The only "hero" in the story is the father. He allowed the prodigal son to try his wings, knowing that it was useless for him to find true joy in any other way. Some people are like that. They have to prove to themselves that all the sinful, shameful, selfish ways the world, the flesh, and the Devil offer us do not satisfy the heart and soul. No one can convince them of it. They have to find out the hard way! But there the Father is, patiently waiting and looking—what a picture of God's mercy!

When he saw the repentant son coming in his ragged disgraceful state, "while he was yet a long way off," the father ran to him and embraced and kissed him. That is how eager and responsive God is to us when we repent for what we are and what we have done against Him.

Your Father's Good Pleasure   February 22

Hebrews 11:1-3, 8-19 and Luke 12:32-40

*Fear not, little flock, for it is your Father's good pleasure
to give you the kingdom.*   Luke 12:32 (rsv)

WHAT ARE THE MOST IMPORTANT THINGS IN LIFE? Jesus
wants us to discern between things that will last and things
that are simply passing away even as we think about them.

In this passage we find His famous word, "Where your
treasure is, there will your heart be also." It's a fact—as we
invest of our treasure our heart will follow. If we give money or
material goods in a certain direction, our interest will follow.

Money and goods are not the only kind of "treasure."
Sometimes we have too much invested in people who are dear
to us. We wrap our lives around them, so we are affected by
their every move or decision. Parents sometimes find it hard to
let their children go, and keep trying to shape their lives even
after they are grown.

Before Jesus says anything about what we ought to do, he
gives us this reassuring word: "Fear not, little flock, it is your
Father's good pleasure to give you the kingdom." He knows
our fears, and does not command us just to give away bravely
or sell what we have.

What Jesus does say is, "Remember, it is your Father's
good pleasure to *give* you the kingdom." God is a giving God.
The Christian life is not made up merely of hard choices and
difficult obedience. It is learning to live in harmony with
God, who loves us infinitely and intimately. It is learning to
choose what is best, because it *is* best and is rooted in His all-
encompassing love for us. He wants to give us the kingdom.
Quite a gift!

To receive this gift, however, we have to let go of those
things that fill up our hands and our hearts and leave no room
for Him. Our worries, our fears, our anger and bitterness leave
no room for His lasting treasures. We must, with His help, get

rid of these things so we can enjoy His gifts more fully.

Let us all pray and ask Him what we're holding onto that keeps us from receiving what it is His *good pleasure* to give us. The exchange will certainly be worth it!

The World Has Gone After Him   FEBRUARY 23

Colossians 1:11-20 and John 12:9-19

The Pharisees said to one another, "You see that you can do nothing. Look, the world has gone after Him."
JOHN 12:19 (RSV)

ISN'T IT STRANGE WHAT JEALOUSY DOES TO OUR VISION? That's what was happening to the Pharisees in this case. They looked at the way people were responding to Jesus and it seemed that "the world" was being won over to His cause. Would that it had been so!

We were talking at our house one evening not long ago, and everyone was sharing their thoughts and feelings of the day. There were several children at the table, and when we had gone all around, I noticed the five-year-old daughter of our guests had been overlooked in the whole conversation. She was waving her hand and wanted to speak. So I said, "Tell us about your day." She smiled and said (with a slight lisp), "I was jealouth at the beach." "You were jealous?" we asked. "Why?" "Becauth," she said, "everyone had a thnorkle but me." We congratulated her on her honesty about her feelings.

Her mother told me later, "Strange thing about that jealousy at the beach. Actually only one child there had a snorkle." But in the little girl's eyes, "Everyone had a thnorkle"but her.

Bad moods can distort the way we perceive reality. When we feel down, or indulge in self-pity, even the slightest thing can hurt our feelings. So it is important to keep from giving in to the ugly, dark feelings that sometimes come upon us. When they

come, we can ask the Lord to show us what they are rooted in—
whether it is fear, anxiety, jealousy or self-pity—and then confess that to the Lord, ask Him to forgive us and give us grace to
get out of the dark mood. It's well worth the effort!

Call to Worship

They that wait upon the Lord shall renew their strength;
they shall mount up with wings as eagles; they shall run and not
be weary; they shall walk and not faint. The Lord is nigh unto
all them that call upon Him, to all that call upon Him in truth.

The Mystery of Suffering   FEBRUARY 24

Job 1:1, 2:1-10 and Mark 10:2-16

*Shall we receive good at the hand of God,
and shall we not receive evil?*   JOB 2:10 (RSV)

"WHY IS THIS HAPPENING TO ME?" Did you ever hear someone
ask that question? Or did you ever ask it yourself? Chances
are that the question referred to something "evil" rather than
"good." It seems human nature to take good for granted and to
think that suffering and tragedy are not supposed to happen to us.

The mystery of suffering has occupied and puzzled some of
the greatest minds. The Book of Job deals with the unparalleled
example of a man who was without fault, according to God's
testimony, a "perfect and upright man" (verse 3) who experiences three major sources of suffering: the loss of his sons and
daughters, the loss of material wealth, and the physical pain of
some loathsome disease. That pretty well sums up the areas of
suffering, so that Job becomes a kind of prototype of someone
who is faced with unexplained suffering.

It is difficult to turn over our thoughts to God when everything is going well with us. It is when our life becomes less
agreeable to us that we become more willing to seek God. What

great humility God has, to take us—even when we have shown that we prefer everything else to Him.

He is willing to take the "left-overs," so to speak.

If you are going through unexplained suffering or a painful experience, it is time to do some of the most important work, inward work, you have ever done in your life. It is time to "get down to business with God." Job took God seriously enough to continue with Him. He chose to believe in God's goodness, and his hope did not die.

The Wounded Healer   FEBRUARY 25

Isaiah 53:7-12 and Mark 10:35-45

He was oppressed, and he was afflicted, yet he opened not his mouth: ISAIAH 53:7A (KJV)

EIGHTEEN OR SO YEARS AGO, ONE OF OUR SONS got into serious trouble with the law. As a pastor, I felt totally exposed and devastated. Aside from my concern for my son, I felt the incident would of necessity wreck any further effectiveness I might have in the church I was serving, so I offered to resign. To shorten a long story, the people responded in a way that amazed me and taught me a great lesson. They expressed compassion, support, and understanding. Their love was nothing short of overwhelming.

Talking the situation over with a close friend, I remarked, "I just don't understand it. These people are more loving to us than they have ever been in all the years we have been here. Why is it?"

My friend smiled and said, "You were never willing to let your *need* show before. You wanted them to think you had it all together."

The incident was crucial in changing my ministry. More people began to come for counseling and help. My wounds—the wounds of our whole family—had somehow made us more accessible to others who were going through trouble themselves.

Our Scriptures talk about Jesus' sufferings, His wounds. He is not above being touched and affected by our problems, our fears and temptations, our sickness and our sorrows because He Himself has been through them. So we do not need to fear that our problems are too petty, that our hurts are too slight, our sins too insignificant to take them to Him.

Today is a good time to test the truth of this great word: "Surely He has borne our griefs and carried our sorrows . . . with His stripes we are healed." Take your burden to Him, whatever it is—your unhappiness, your resentments, your hurts, your frustrations, your crabbiness, your temptations. Whatever your burden is, He knows. He understands and He is willing to speak peace to your soul.

Faith: The Fruit of Obedience   FEBRUARY 26

Isaiah 62:1-5 and John 2:1-11

His mother said to the servants, "Do whatever He tells you."
JOHN 2:5 (RSV)

JOHN HAS RECORDED FOR US THE FIRST OF JESUS' "SIGNS," which He did at Cana in Galilee. In doing so, He has taught us how faith and obedience fit together. Jesus is attending a wedding reception with His disciples. Unfortunately, the wine has run out, and Mary, the mother of our Lord, knows of the predicament. After talking with Jesus, she gives succinct directions to the servants: *"Do whatever He tells you."*

As Christians we are to do whatever He tells us. This truth applies to each and every follower of Jesus Christ, whatever the status or condition. Not all are called to preach great messages; not all are called to lead numbers of people; not all are called to bear heavy burdens. In specific calls, the people of God diverge according to the variety of their gifts. But all of us begin from the same starting point: "Do whatever He tells you."

The servants did as Jesus told them and John concludes the story by saying, *"And his disciples believed in Him." (John 2:11)* Their increased faith was the direct result of the obedience of the servants.

What is God telling us through this reading? Perhaps the present circumstances of your life have weakened your faith. Or, perhaps you know God is asking you to do something, but you are not sure that your faith is strong enough. To each of our circumstances, the wedding at Cana brings a word of encouragement. Faith is the fruit of obedience.

Let us determine today to do whatever we know God is telling us to do. God's word assures us that Jesus will take our step of obedience and transform it into the sweet nectar of faith. Then we may find that the greatest miracle of Christ's glory will be the change that takes place within our own hearts.

Paul's Testimony—And Ours   February 27

Luke 8:9-14 and II Timothy 4:6-8

*I have fought the good fight, I have finished the race,
I have kept the faith.* II Tim. 4:7 (rsv)

KNOWING THE TIME WAS DRAWING NEAR for his departure from the Christian struggle, Paul wrote this letter from prison to his spiritual son, Timothy. And he sums up his life in these three simple statements.

I have fought the good fight. We Christians must be reminded over and over that the spiritual life is a battle, a struggle. Temptations and trials are a natural and inevitable part of being human. But we can make the struggle and suffering redemptive by letting God use them to train and mature us. Paul did that. We are still in process—but the challenge remains: "Fight the good fight."

I have finished the race. Probably we've all been counseled by our parents, "Don't be a quitter!" My mother used to say: "If a task is once begun, never leave it till it's done. Be the labor great or small, do it well or not at all." Have you seen the thousands in the New York or Boston marathons? The goal for the majority of them is just to cross the finish line.

Do you find your life at a point at which you are tempted to give up, get discouraged, become "faithless"? Do you lack belief that God will continue to do a good work in your life? Are you discouraged, depressed or full of self-pity? Look at Paul, writing from prison, and determine to finish the race you started.

Finally, he says, *I have kept the faith.* What did that mean to him? It meant not denying Jesus, even when threatened with death. Our struggle is against everything in us that would tempt us to be untrue to God, to the truth we know. Our struggle is to allow the truth to set us free from foolish fears and anxieties. God is still on His throne. He is still worthy of our trust. He is still able to save those who call upon Him. Keep that faith in your heart. Let it be your strength when days are dark, and you cannot see what the future holds. Remember what someone has said, "I do not know what the future holds, but I know who holds the future." Keep the faith!

The Bothersome Widow   FEBRUARY 28

II Tim 3:14-4:5 and Luke 18:1-8

And he told them a parable, to the effect that they ought always to pray and not to lose heart. LUKE 18:1 (RSV)

IN THE STORY OF THE BOTHERSOME WIDOW and the crooked judge, we have a man who "neither feared God nor regarded man." He had seen so much need that he had long since closed his heart to it. But the widow had a need so pressing that she would not forget it. She could not rest until the matter was settled. So her need drove her again and again to the hardhearted judge.

Jesus is telling us how important it is to keep on praying. Too often we make our little prayer, and if God doesn't rush to answer it, we suppose He doesn't hear or doesn't care, or "prayer doesn't work." And that is Jesus' point. We cannot afford to let the delay put us off. If that judge finally said in exasperation, "Though I neither fear God nor man, yet because this widow bothers me, I will vindicate her," what does that say about a loving God? Jesus says, "If that is true about that unrighteous judge, will not God vindicate His elect who cry to Him day and night?" How is that vindication shown? By hearing and answering our prayer!

The worldly minded cannot understand the spiritual man or woman. We believe in a God who cannot be seen and a way of life that must be followed by faith. We are burdened with concerns that make no sense to those who do not take God seriously. Like the needy widow, we must again and again go to the Lord with our own spiritual needs, sins, and failures, and our concerns about those we love.

God's unfathomable love is greater than our need. Though He may wait to answer our prayer, the delay has a purpose. And part of that purpose is to clarify and purify our asking. But never does the delay mean that God has turned a deaf ear to our prayer. Unanswered prayers are testing places. They not only test our faith, they test our willingness to persist in what we believe is a good request. Like the woman who said, "If I can but touch the hem of His garment, I shall be made whole," we are invited to reach out—and keep on reaching out.

How God Humbles Us FEBRUARY 29

I Thessalonians 2:1-13, 17-20 and Matthew 23:1-12

. . . whoever exalts himself will be humbled, and whoever humbles himself will be exalted. MATTHEW 23:12 (RSV)

THIS WORD OF JESUS ALWAYS SOUNDED like a threat as I read it, a warning not to exalt myself. We may take pride in our honesty or truthfulness, or our record of never having shirked at work or cheated at school. We may take pride in our family background, or our church identity. When we allow those good things to lift us above others "less fortunate" than ourselves, we are guilty of exalting ourselves.

But we should look at this verse in its positive light. It is a promise that if we willingly humble ourselves, we will be exalted in due time. But it is a promise, too, that if we exalt ourselves, God, in His great mercy, will humble us. That may be painful, but it is not *bad.*

First, He humbles us by allowing us to come to the end of our self-chosen way. The prodigal son in Jesus' parable was a willful, proud young man who demanded his share of his father's estate and went off to waste it all. In the end he was feeding pigs, a painful disgrace to any Jewish mind, and further, he was even willing to eat the pigs' food.

Second, God humbles us by allowing the things we have taken such pride in to fade away. A beautiful young woman who is too vain may see herself growing old, and to her eyes, unattractive. We are humbled by the aging process. Having to come to grips that we could not achieve all we had dreamed of can also humble us in a good and healthy sense, and make us more merciful toward others.

Finally, He humbles us by letting us see how vain we really are inside, and by giving us a good look at our real selves. He allows us to take ourselves less seriously. Genuine self-knowledge brings genuine humility. This is all for our good, our peace of mind, and our ultimate happiness.

The God of All Comfort

*Praise be to the God and
Father of our Lord Jesus Christ,
the Father of compassion and
the God of all comfort,
who comforts us in all our
troubles, so that we can
comfort those in any trouble
with the comfort we ourselves
have received from God.*

II COR. 1:3 (NIV)

The Seven Joys of Being a Grandparent

The picture I had of being a grandparent was one of dignity, sitting by a fire in a rocker smoking a pipe or knitting a shawl. I could never understand older people cooing and goo-gooing over babies who were spitting and throwing up all over them. So much for preconceived notions! I'm sure I wouldn't believe it if someone put a "hidden camera" on me now that I am a grandmother for the second time.

The first joy of being a grandparent is a second chance. I loved our one and only daughter, but I cannot say I enjoyed her youth very much for fear of having to be the perfect mother. Now I can gaze at this newborn miracle of a grandchild without a worry in the world and just marvel at God's creation in this tiny form.

The second joy of being a grandparent is the vision of what it's like to be totally dependent on God. Kate never looks anxious or worries about how she will be taken care of. She lets her needs be made known loud and clear! (Hers are very simple—why are mine so complicated?) As long as she eats, sleeps, and stays clean, she is happy as can be!

The third joy of being a grandparent is the glimpse of heaven that it gives me. Who is Kate cooing at and smiling for? (Out of the mouths of babes and sucklings has thou ordained strength . . . Psalm 8:2.) I know angels are surrounding her tiny body. Is she sitting on Jesus' lap or frolicking with one of his lambs?

The fourth joy of being a grandparent is that my myopic vision is expanded and transformed. The other day I took our older granddaughter (two and a half) to the beach. We came across a tidal pool. I saw still murky water, pieces of debris trapped on the bottom, pollen covering the top, slimy little fish, broken shells that hurt my feet. She saw a "swimming pool." She squealed every time she saw a fish. She delighted in splashing the murky water. She tried to pick up each shell and wanted to take them home as treasures to show proudly to Mom and Dad.

What else am I not seeing with the delights of a child's eyes?

The fifth joy of being a grandparent is the quality time I am able to have with my grandchildren, because I am not exhausted from taking care of children all day long, doing housework, cooking meals, and holding down a job as well.

The sixth joy of being a grandparent is that the empty nest does not stay empty too long. Just as the children fly the coop, little "sparrows" come to take their place. And furthermore, I have to take care of myself and stay young, so I will have the energy to do my part of grandparenting!

Lastly, the seventh joy of being a grandmother is the unconditional love I am given. I am just loved for who I am. I don't think too many children wish they had different grandparents, but plenty would trade parents if they could.

I have listed the seven joys that come to mind. I'm sure every grandparent can list seventy times seven!

Barbara Manuel

But at Your Word

I Corinthians 15:1-11 and Luke 5: 1-11

Master, we toiled all night and took nothing!
But at your word I will let down the nets. LUKE 5:5 (RSV)

PETER, AS HE SO OFTEN DOES, EXPRESSES the kind of feelings we all have. He and his friends have done their best. They have "toiled all night." It must have been a frustrating experience. When you think about it, that's true of so many things in life. We set out with the best intentions, throw a lot of energy and effort into something, only to find it doesn't produce the desired results. And so we "come back to shore," so to speak, discouraged and disappointed. Has life brought you to such a time when you feel your efforts have proven fruitless? Have you "toiled all night" and felt that you have caught nothing?

We can choose to stay in the disappointment and frustration, or we can hear what this word is saying to us. Shall we look at the night's toil and its lack, or shall we look at this day and its opportunities? Never mind the disappointments of the past. Never mind the hurts we sustained, the hopes that got dashed when things didn't "work out right." They belong to the "night" in which we toiled and caught nothing. There is a new word for today: "Cast your nets out into the deep." Let your present situation give you courage to venture in faith to a new and better relationship with your heavenly Father. That's what "casting your nets into the deep" means for many of us. We have played it safe, perhaps kept God at arm's length. Somehow we survived the disappointments and the griefs. But there is something better. God wants us nearer Him. He wants us to be His own in ways where we have been too busy before. In spite all the accumulated doubts we have brought out of the night of toil—we can say, "Nevertheless, at your word we will." He is waiting to bless that choice. Don't miss the blessing!

For Me to Live is Christ   MARCH 2

Philippians 1:21-27 and Matthew 20:1-16

For to me, to live is Christ and to die is gain.
PHILIPPIANS 1:21 (NIV)

PAUL IS WRITING HERE ABOUT THE UNCERTAINTY of his life. Now, no one likes to dwell morbidly on how frail life is and how uncertain it is. In fact, there are few subjects less talked about than death. But when John Donne wrote these famous lines of his, he spoke for us all:

No man is an island, entire of itself,
every man is a piece of the continent, part of the main;
if a clod be washed away by the sea, Europe is the less,
as well as if a promontory were,
as well as if a manor of thy friends or of thine own were;
any man's death diminishes me,
because I am involved in mankind;
and therefore never send to know for whom
the bell tolls: it tolls for thee.

(From *Devotions, XVII*)

In this passage, Paul is looking back across his life and thinking about what it has meant. There are times when we also may think we have done our duty and run the course, and we may wonder of what possible use can we be now. Yet I can say that I have learned more from those who had reached their senior years than from any others—more about life in its fullness. The latter years are meant to be a blessing, not only to those who are allowed to "grow old," but through them to the generations still coming along.

There are many ways we can be a blessing—if our heart attitude is right. Paul knew it from the Roman jail: "For me to live is Christ." There is no sad end to a life that is so full of the love and blessing of God. Only "to die is gain." May it be so for all of us, when our work is done.

Hope in God   MARCH 3

Psalm 42 and 43 and John 17:20-26

Why are you cast down, O my soul, and why are you disquieted within me? Hope in God; for I shall again praise him, my help and my God. PSALM 43:5 (RSV)

ALEXANDER MACLAREN, the great ninteenth-century preacher, says about the Psalms, that they read like the sob of a wounded heart. The psalmist "is shut out from the temple of his God, from the holy soil of his native land. One can see him sitting solitary yonder in the lonely wilderness . . . with a longing, wistful gaze, yearning across the narrow valley and the rushing stream that lay between him and the land of God's chosen people; and his eye resting perhaps on the mountain top that looked down on Jerusalem . . . He was depressed because he was shut out from the tokens of God's presence [the temple], and because he was depressed, he shut himself out from the *reality* of God's presence."

The key is in the last sentence: Because the psalmist was depressed, he shut himself out from the presence of God. That is the experience of many of us. We allow our *feelings* to act as though they were the final word, and assume that they are telling us the truth about our situation and about God. Then we deny ourselves the very Power that could bring us out of our depression and into the sunlight of God.

One of the most important things we can do when we find ourselves in self-pity is to begin to take steps to get out of it. We can, by the grace and power of Jesus Christ, get up and *do* something about it. We can sing a hymn; we can praise God out loud; we can begin to memorize some Scripture or some great poem or other thought. If we find unconfessed sin within us, making us guilty, we can confess it and accept forgiveness. Too often we don't go the final step of accepting the forgiveness and cleansing which is ours when we repent. Afterwards, we can set our faces to go on with Jesus as obediently as we can.

What Manner of Love   MARCH 4

I John 3:1-7

See what love the Father has given us, that we should
be called the children of God; and so we are.   I JOHN 3:1 (RSV)

WE HEAR A LOT OF TALK TODAY about "loving yourself,"
and "accepting yourself." Jesus recognized that we do
love ourselves, and cautioned us to "love your neighbor as
yourself." But that is a far different thing from learning to
accept and believe in God's amazing love for us. Once we get
honest with ourselves, and face up to how far short we fall of
what we should be and want to be, it becomes easy to feel that
God must not like us very much. That kind of thinking can lead
to a kind of hardening of the surface of our hearts, so that we
feel neither very lovable nor very loving. These feelings can
become a prison to us.

John was writing to people who have all the same feelings
and problems we do. And what he says to them applies equally
to us. Yet John says that we are now children of God. We are
not just accidents cast up on the surface of time and chance. We
are beloved souls. God deeply cares for you and me, and has set
His love upon us. That can and should make a difference in the
way we approach life.

Think of it this way: a child comes into the world and is
loved, not because of anything he or she does, but because the
child belongs to the mother and father. It is a picture of the
grace and goodness of God, that without our earning it or
doing anything about it, we are beloved children of our heavenly Father.

If we are children of God, then we have a Father who can
help us in our need. If we are children of God, we have a model,
an example to help us know how to face life. Jesus faced more
problems than any of us can imagine, and He was faithful. With
His help we can face all the problems that come to us, and we
can be faithful, too. We can come out of our self-imposed prisons

and greet life with hope and a smile—*because* we are children of our heavenly Father. Let's claim that birthright today.

A God Who Cares   MARCH 5

Acts 13:15-16, 26-33, Revelation 7:9-17, and John 10:22-30

And God will wipe away every tear from their eyes.
REVELATION 7:17B (RSV)

WHAT AN UNFORGETTABLE SCENE in Revelation, chapter 7! Myriads of people from every tribe and tongue shout and sing praises to God and to the Lamb.

They are those who have endured great trouble while on earth. They have dipped their robes in suffering like that of Jesus Himself, and their robes, like His, are now glistening white. This is a different way of looking at the tribulations of life. What made such difficulties a means of cleansing the soul?—They bore them for Him.

Recently I heard this story: A group of martyrs arrived at the gate to the Beloved Country. The guardian said to them, "God has given much to you. Have you brought any gift to Him?" "Only our pain," said the martyrs, "and that is nothing compared to Christ's sufferings for us." "It is a good gift," said the guardian, "and you are doubly welcome as comrades of the cross."

However bitter the things we must face in this earthly journey, God sees, God knows, God remembers. Even pain we cannot alleviate can be an offering to Him.

But it is at the end of this chapter that we meet the most striking part of the scene. Can you remember when you were young and hurt yourself, or got into a fight with someone, or felt awful over something, and you began to cry, and your mother took a handkerchief and wiped away the tears from your eyes? Somehow you just felt better after that, even though nothing else had changed. Knowing she cared made the problem seem more tolerable.

Here is the Almighty Father of all creation, praised by unnumbered throngs, taking each of us like little hurt children, and wiping every tear away. Such is the tender love and mercy of our God to us. Such is the destiny that awaits His children. And this glimpse of it is meant to strengthen us, encourage our patience, and renew our desire to be more like Him. It is the picture of those who have forgotten to be sad.

So let us be cheerful, even now, knowing that the God who cares so much is our daily Companion, closer than breathing, nearer than hands and feet. His strength and comfort are ours if we will have them!

He Will Rejoice Over You   MARCH 6

Zephaniah 3:14-20 and Luke 3:7-18

The Lord thy God in the midst of thee is mighty: He will save,
He will rejoice over thee with joy: He will rest in His love;
He will joy over thee with singing. ZEPHANIAH 3:17 (KJV)

ZEPHANIAH PROPHESIED and wrote when the nation of Judah was nearing its close. He foresaw that the land would be devastated under the righteous judgment of the Lord but that God would yet bring Judah back and would restore her in His own time and way. This word is also for us, and there are a number of encouraging lessons for us.

First, God is greater than the circumstances around us. He is able to save to the uttermost those who put their trust in Him. He is a God who hears and answers prayers. Therefore we are bidden to make our petitions known to Him. The answer is sure—not always just the way we like, and not always when we would like; but He is faithful and will answer our cry for help. A childlike trust is the key to His heart.

Second, God says He will rejoice in us. That's a breathtaking thought. The God who made everything, who is so great that we cannot begin to encompass Him with our minds, will rejoice over His people. It is a part of His great kindness and generosity that He has created us and made us objects of His love and joy. We know that as human beings we find joy in those we love. We love to give them gifts. We rejoice in their good health and their successes.

We have to ask ourselves, how can we live today in the present circumstances of our lives in a way that God can truly rejoice over us? Can we bear our burdens cheerfully? Can we offer up simple prayer for those needy and hurting places we know of? I believe that we have the privilege of adding to God's joy—as fantastic and unbelievable as that sounds!

Prayer

With thankfulness for Your gracious promises, heavenly Father, may we bring joy to Your heart through our glad obedience to Your Word; through Jesus Christ our Lord. Amen.

God's Word Abides MARCH 7

I Thessalonians 2:1-13, 17-20 and Matthew 23:1-12

. . . when you received the word of God, you accepted it not as the word of men, but as what it really is, the word of God, which is at work in you believers. I THESS. 2:13 (RSV)

THERE ARE NOT MANY THINGS IN THIS WORLD that do abide. The hymn writer, Rev. Henry Lyte, said, "Change and decay in all around I see." Life is a continual change. We look for the old landmarks, and often they have disappeared. Even morals we were taught are now being called into question. Change is everywhere.

Not all change is bad! I'm glad that I lived at a time when

heart by pass surgery was available as a relatively safe procedure. Some changes have relieved us of many a pain and discomfort, so we can be thankful for them.

But life needs abiding stability. We can't live in a constantly
changing world with no fixed points. Sanity and peace of mind
require that some things *do not change*. And that is what
Luther was celebrating in his immortal hymn based on Psalm
46: "A mighty fortress is our God, a *bulwark* never failing."
Those strong words in the last stanza have been a support and
encouragement to many a weatherworn soul in the centuries
since it was written. "That word [meaning God's Word], above
all earthly powers, no thanks to them abideth."

Each day, as we turn to the words of Holy Scripture, God
speaks anew to our need. It doesn't matter how many times we
have read it before, as the Spirit quickens it to our hearts, it
meets our present need. That is the miracle of His abiding
Word. Perhaps you know that even verses you learned as a child
linger on, and become life-giving as you think of them. How
greatly we are loved, knowing that our God, who is the same
yesterday, today, and forever, has given us His abiding Word.
May it bring you joy and encouragement day by day.

God is Our Comfort   MARCH 8

Isaiah 66:10-14 and Luke 10:1-11, 16-20

*As one whom a mother comforts, so I will comfort you; you
shall be comforted in Jerusalem.*   ISAIAH 66:13 (RSV)

IN THIS LAST CHAPTER OF THE BOOK OF ISAIAH, the prophet
assures God's people that He knows their situation and that
He cares. The Book of Isaiah contains some very severe judg-
ments and warnings. But at the fortieth chapter, the tone
changes. It seems evident that the Jewish people were under
oppression and needed some words of assurance and hope.

That is God's way. When we are rebellious and willful, He utters strong warnings. They are warnings of love because our rebellion bears bitter consequences, sometimes going on from generation to generation. So, stern and severe warnings are not a sign of rejection but of fatherly care.

But there comes a time when we need another tone of voice. We need a tender word of assurance, for we may have hardened ourselves against Him. "As one whom his mother comforts" changes the figure considerably. You can almost visualize the little child running with a scratch or cut or bruise, and its mother not only treating it, but soothing with words and perhaps a hug.

At the later stages of life we have to face some pretty serious problems. It may be a deterioration of health. There may be a whole battery of new pains and aches with which we have to deal. It may be the loss of freedom of movement, and we may find ourself limited, either by bodily pain or by circumstance. What can we do in these cases? We can do what the child does when he hurts and feels frightened. We can go to Him who "comforts as his mother comforts." This is no imaginary fantasy, but a living, caring Father who welcomes our coming with our need.

Today, if you are in need of comfort, do not hesitate to hasten to your heavenly Father. If you see others in need, encourage them to do the same. With His comfort we can become channels of the same comfort to others around us.

Striving to Enter Rest   MARCH 9

Isaiah 53:4-12 and Hebrews 4:9-16

Let us therefore strive to enter that rest   HEBREWS 4:11A (RSV)

TODAY'S TEXT POINTS US beyond the "labors" of today. And even though we may be in a time of life when the greatest labor we have is not to become bored with inactivity, it is still an important word. For the rest he is talking about is something more than physical rest from hard work.

He is speaking of soul rest. We are not at rest in our souls when we are dissatisfied and unhappy. We are not at rest when we harbor feelings of fear and anxiety, worrying about what might happen tomorrow. We could name many other attitudes which rob us of rest for our souls. And we must admit, honestly, that all of us endure much unrest of mind and spirit, because we do not always strive against these negative feelings. So we are counselled, "Strive to enter that rest."

He is speaking of a God-given rest. It is not something we invent. It is something which our Creator has prepared for us. It is real, not something we imagine or talk ourselves into. So it is worth seeking, striving for. Jesus said, "Come to me, all who labor and are heavy-laden, and I will give you rest." He keeps His word. He will not fail us. Begin to fight against the falsehoods that would rob you of faith and convince you that life is all dark and gloomy. Don't concentrate and linger on things that drag you down, but turn your inward eyes towards heaven, and "ask, and it shall be given; seek and you shall find; knock, and it shall be opened unto you."

He is speaking of a growing rest. It is not a static, passive thing. It is a state of mind and heart intended to grow until it reaches its fulfillment in heaven. This life is not the whole story. It is a wonderful part of the story, and we should treasure it, but it is not complete. It points toward a fuller, richer, "more restful" life beyond. At any rate, this life is meant to be a preparing time, a growing time, a "striving time," looking forward to that perfect rest which awaits those who have won it.

And I Will Make it Known MARCH 10

Acts 16:16-34, Revelation 22:12-17, and John 17:20-26

*O righteous Father . . . I made known to them Thy name, and I
will make it known, that the love with which Thou hast loved
me may be in them and I in them.*   JOHN 17:26 (RSV)

JESUS IS ABOUT TO LEAVE HIS LITTLE GROUP of disciples. He
loves them very much. They have been the first to believe in
Him, and they have left much to go with Him as He travelled
up and down Galilee, Judea—and even Samaria (which most
Jews avoided like a plague) teaching and preaching that the
Kingdom of heaven was at hand and inviting people to repent
of their old attitudes and to begin to believe God in a new way.
He loved those men and the women who ministered to all of
them as they went about healing and teaching. They were His
special friends, and He knew that what was just ahead would
be a very hard test for them. So He prayed for them. But He
also prayed for us. "I pray . . . for those who are to believe in
Me through their word." That's you and me and all of us who
believe in Him today. He had us in His heart as He prayed.

He is summing up His life and mission. He says, "I made
known Your name to them . . ." Making known God's "name"
meant revealing the nature of God in a new and fuller way. We
know God differently, more deeply, more intimately because of
what Jesus made known about Him.

That isn't the end, though. He says, "And I will make it
known." That looked ahead—to the cross and resurrection,
certainly—when God took our sin and guilt upon Himself and
"reconciled the world to Himself," when God declared that
death does not have the final word—but that Life is His final
word to us.

And even beyond that: Jesus is making known who God is
right now for you and me in our daily lives. You may think your
life is pretty insignificant. You may even be annoyed by many

unavoidable things in your life at present. And you may look back across your life with no great sense of achievement. But remember this: right now Jesus Christ is busy making God's nature, His very Heart known to you, if you are open to Him. Don't close Him off or think that it's all a waste of time. Talk to Him and listen in your heart for His words of comfort, hope, and love.

All Loves Excelling   MARCH 11

I Corinthians 13:1-13

So faith, hope, love abide, these three; but the greatest of these is love.   I COR. 13:13 (RSV)

WHEN WESLEY WROTE THIS HYMN in 1747, he used the plural "loves" in the first line. "Love divine, *all loves excelling.*" Have you ever thought about the different loves in your life, the different ways and degrees in which you love?

We are greatly affected by what we love. People who "love money" are fraught with many cares, stresses, and disappointments. People who love fame find that no fame is great enough to satisfy their need.

There is also the love of *things.* All too many of us know what that kind of love can do—it can drive us to cling even to small things as though they gave meaning to our lives. It can make us unwilling to share what we have with others. Not a nice kind of love, really.

Then there is love of family and friends. That's good—a noble kind of love, if it does not insist on being the *most* important thing in our lives. Even family and friends cannot be God, and God is jealous of His rightful place in our hearts. So even the best human love can be a danger if it is not submitted to the greater love of God.

Paul is talking to the Christians at Corinth about a different kind of love. It is the love they have received from God through their faith in Jesus Christ. He describes it in rather careful detail in this thirteenth chapter of I Corinthians. It is the kind of love that caused God to send His Son to be our Savior, and to love us in spite of all our unloveableness. Maybe you have had people who loved you "in spite of who you were." I know I have!

No Longer a Slave but a Son   MARCH 12

John 1:1-18 and Galatians 3:29—4:7

And because you are sons, God has sent the Spirit of His Son into our hearts, crying, "Abba! Father!" So through God you are no longer a slave but a son, and if a son then an heir.
GAL. 4:6,7 (RSV)

IS GOD'S LOVE REAL TO YOU? Many of us know in our heads that God loves us—but His love is not an ever-present reality.

This has been true with me when facing pain and illness. Encountering a new symptom, I tend to hunker down and endure, feeling alone and apprehensive about what might come next. Instead of running to the heavenly Father and leaning more closely upon Him, I tend to withdraw into myself. You may not be totally unlike me!

Paul knew what it was to suffer. He faced physical suffering, a permanent "thorn in the flesh" which did not go away when he prayed about it. He faced hostility and hatred, and saw his name "cast out as evil." He also faced ingratitude and controversy among the very people he had sacrificed to help. But here, talking to some of those very people, he says, "God has sent the Spirit of His Son into our hearts." Paul *knew* that God loved him.

How can we have that experiential knowledge that goes deeper than head knowledge? John Wesley preached for years before feeling his heart "strangely warmed," and then became a flame of truth and hope for hundreds of thousands of people. We must *want* to sense the love of God more deeply. We must not be content to face our problems with stoic resignation. However serious, our problems are meant to draw us closer to God's heart.

He really does love you and me. He has sent His beloved Son to save us and claim us for Himself. And He has sent His Spirit into our hearts to "shed abroad the love of God." The Spirit is the Spirit of "sonship," meaning the spirit of a child's love for our parents, whether we are sons or daughters. It is a bonding, trusting, strengthening love. Who can separate us from the love of God?

Let the Spirit touch your heart deeply, and warm it with God's love for you and with your love for Him. We are no longer slaves, but children of God.

The Passing and the Permanent   MARCH 13

Isaiah 51:1-6 and John 6:60-69

For the heavens will vanish with smoke, the earth will wear out like a garment, and they who dwell in it will die like gnats, but my salvation will be forever, and my deliverance will never be ended.   ISAIAH 51:6B (RSV)

The words that I have spoken to you are spirit and life.   JOHN 6:63B (RSV)

FROM TIME TO TIME I AM REMINDED of how a childhood illusion of the "firm earth" (*terra firma*) has been shattered by repeated assertions that any part of the earth is subject to earthquakes.

There are some other "certainties" that seem also to be shaken or shaking. The permanence of marriage was a part of my "mental furniture." People got married to *stay* married. It was part of the stability of life. But then, seeing the breakup of the homes of many, many people whom I loved, I began to see how truly *unstable* is the human commitment to "love, honor, and cherish till death us do part."

I'm sure any of us could name other things that don't seem as firm and permanent as they used to be. The Bible is full of reminders that "Man that is born of woman is of few days, and full of trouble. He comes forth like a flower, and withers; he flees like a shadow, and continues not." (Job 14:1, 2) Our sojourn here is a limited one. We are not permanent residents of this fair earth. This is difficult to comprehend emotionally.

Now I do not entirely welcome the thought of saying farewell to this world but it is a world that must and will pass away. John saw " a new heaven and a new earth, for the first heaven and the first earth had passed away." (Rev. 21:1) This being the case, we are foolish to let our hearts cling to this earth when God is calling us to something higher and better. He invites us to look beyond and let all the experiences here prepare our hearts for what He has in store for His people.

Jesus echoed these words from Isaiah when He said, "Heaven and earth shall pass away, but my words shall never pass away." "Come to me," He said, "all who labor and are heavy-laden, and I will give you rest." "The words that I have spoken to you are spirit and life." *That* life will never pass away.

The Wideness of His Mercy   MARCH 14

Deuteronomy 26:1-11 and Romans 10: 8B-13

The same Lord is Lord of all and bestows his riches upon all who call upon him. For, "everyone who calls upon the name of the Lord will be saved." ROMANS 10:12B, 13 (RSV)

GOD'S LOVE IS SO GREAT THAT WE CANNOT even adequately express it when we talk with one another. However, that does not mean that He is indifferent to sin. Sin is what separates us from him, and it is such a serious malady that God sent his only begotten Son to deal with it. Jesus Christ lived and died in order to bring healing to our souls and restoration of a wholesome relationship between us and God. He is our Bridge, our Reconciler, our Redeemer. His work has transformed the world—especially transforming those who believe in him.

But His mercy is wider than ours and His love overflows the boundaries that we place around it. He loves the ugly, the unlovable, the person we find it almost impossible to love.

Today we have the opportunity to see and rejoice in the wideness of God's mercy—to us and to others who are not like us. We have the opportunity to pray for those who seem to be blind to him, and whose lives are torn in pieces by their wrong choices. We can either look at them and say, "Thank God I'm not like *that.*" Or we can look at them and say, "They too are beloved of God. God have mercy on them."

In so doing, our hearts grow a little "wider," and our prayer can become a small channel by which God, in His great love, can send blessing where it is sorely needed.

The Mystery of God's Will   MARCH 15

Psalm 24 and Ephesians 1:3-14

For He has made known to us in all wisdom and insight the mystery of His will, according to His good purpose which He set forth in Christ. EPHESIANS 1:9 (RSV)

PAUL HERE TALKS ABOUT "THE MYSTERY OF GOD'S WILL" which has been revealed in these last times. The mystery involved the coming of God's eternal Son, Jesus Christ, to win a people for Him and to bear the sin of the world to the cross. No matter how much has been thought or written about it, it remains a mystery.

First of all, there is the mystery of God's infinite love. We humans would long since have written off the whole human race as a "lost cause," because as a people we are so perverse and foolish. Even as this is written we are astonished at reports of child molestation and abuse, of cruel attacks on unarmed civilians in several countries, and of the seemingly unsolvable disputes between races and ethnic groups—each of which has a water-tight argument for being right. Yet God still loves. God still seeks. He has not given up on us!

Then there is the mystery of what God plans for the future. We cannot know what the future holds for any of us. But if we believe in Jesus Christ, we can be absolutely sure that God's plan is for all things to be gathered in Him in the end.

For Christians, God's promise is: Everything sad will become untrue. Why? Because God so loved us that He sent His Son to save us. Jesus Christ is alive, working by the Holy Spirit to mold and shape us for that future God has prepared for us.

God's love is greater than any circumstance we face. God's care for you is "to the uttermost." He will not fail you and will never let you down. It is His good pleasure to give you the Kingdom. Believe it and rejoice in it every day.

The Appropriate Thing MARCH 16

I Kings 17:17-24, Galatians 1:11-24, and Luke 7:11-17

And when the Lord saw her, he had compassion on her, and said to her, "Do not weep." LUKE 7:13 (RSV)

TODAY'S GOSPEL WAS READ at the funeral of my wife's mother more than twenty years ago, and the minister spoke on it in a way that I have never forgotten. First, let me tell you about my mother-in-law. Several years before her death, she had become very ill with complications of diabetes. Her sight was almost gone. Premature hardening of the arteries caused her to get very confused and to have terrible nightmares, worrying about her grandchildren. All efforts to relieve such distress were but temporary and short-lived. Much of the time she did not know where she was, and when she did, she would cry in her unhappiness. Although she was receiving loving care from her family, her pastor, and her church, she was unable to achieve any sort of stable happiness.

Knowing all this, the minister read the story of the widow of Nain. In that case, Jesus had "interrupted the funeral," so to speak, and raised her son up and restored him to his mother. For them, said the minister, "Jesus did the appropriate thing." Then he made this application: For our mother, He had also done the right thing. For one person, it was to restore earthly life, for the other, it was to relieve suffering and distress. Who could dispute the truth of what he said?

Do you have a circumstance in your life you think is just too awful for words? Is there a physical condition that troubles you and threatens to undermine your cheerfulness and enthusiasm for life? Do you find yourself in circumstances that easily depress you? If such is your case, today's message has a special meaning. God is not unaware of where we are, what we are, and the condition we are in. And God always does the appropriate thing. The thing that will ultimately be best, most fitting, most beneficial for your welfare and mine. Why? Because He cares. Because He loves you. Because He wants only your best—not only for the present moment, but for eternity. That's worth thinking over.

Strengthened to Endure   MARCH 17

Colossians 1:1-14 and Luke 10:25-37

May you be strengthened with all power, according to His glorious might, for all endurance and patience with joy, giving thanks to the Father. . . . COLOSSIANS 1:11, 12A (RSV)

FEW THINGS ARE MORE DISCOURAGING than to be told "cheer up" when we are anything but cheerful, or "be brave" when we are afraid! Can we will ourselves to stop feeling sad or fearful? Not in my experience!

One thing I learned when coming out of open heart surgery and still feeling some effects from the trauma was that I wanted to think I was above fear, and I wanted to convince others that I felt no fear. But my wife, who spent many hours with me during this time, would detect that I was really experiencing fear. She would say to me, "I can see you're afraid, and you need to confess your fear to the Lord and ask Him to help you." I wanted to "hang tough," but she was so persistent that I finally did as she suggested. I prayed, "Lord, I'm afraid. I'm sorry that I'm afraid, because that means I do not trust You as I ought. Please forgive my fear, and let me know Your peace. I accept Your forgiveness, and thank You for it." Peace would come, as I relaxed in the reality of my own need and God's sufficiency. After this happened several times, I learned something about how we handle life's difficulties. In our pride we try to handle them in our own strength—even though strength may have gone out of us for the moment!

> Oh, what peace we often forfeit,
> Oh, what needless pain we bear,
> All because we do not carry
> Everything to God in prayer!

Paul told the Colossians they did not have to pretend to be stronger than they were. They were just ordinary people facing a difficult time. But—oh, the beauty of Paul's prayer for them, that they would be strengthened according to His glorious might. They didn't have to be strong—they had a strong God! They didn't have to pretend to be more than they were—it was all right to admit their weaknesses. Jesus Christ with all His glorious power was present within them. They could call on Him. They could flee to Him. In His glorious might they could find strength to endure. And so can we!

Starting Over   MARCH 18

II Corinthians 5:17-21 and Luke 15:11-32

Therefore, if anyone is in Christ, he is a new creation; the old has passed away, behold the new has come.   II COR. 5:17 (RSV)

WE ALL KNOW WHAT IT IS TO MAKE A DECISION we later regret. The parable of the Prodigal Son tells of a young man's regrettable decision, and the wonderful opportunity afforded him to start over.

Any parent knows the expectations and hopes we pin upon our children. The prodigal's father undoubtedly did the same, but he also allowed for the exercise of his sons' free will. The younger took advantage of that gift and used it to obtain "freedom." He left home with all that was rightfully his—except for wisdom to know how to use it. We can imagine the hurt the father felt. Was he tempted to reject his son, determining never to receive him back?

The day came, however, when this self-loving young man began to grow up. He humbled himself with the thought that perhaps he could return home—as a servant! Filled with uncertainty, he journeyed home, expecting nothing, hoping just for food and shelter.

You know the feeling. When was the last time you swallowed your pride in order to tell someone you were sorry for something you had said or done? Did you wonder if you would be forgiven? Did you expect the relationship would never be the same?

The prodigal son had a surprise in store. He expected little, but his father gave much. The son felt their relationship had ended, but the father imparted the most wonderful of gifts—the opportunity to start over. He received him not as a servant, but fully as his son, celebrating his return as if he had been resurrected from the dead!

Today, no matter who you are or what you have done, God *your* Father is giving you the opportunity to start fresh. Yesterday's sins and errors are past; today His mercies are new! Or is there someone in your life who needs the chance to start over with you? With mercy and forgiveness, can you give that gift? Or maybe you have distanced yourself from a friend or a family member, and you need the opportunity to start over.

For all, the message of the Prodigal Son holds forth hope. In Christ, "the old has passed away, behold the new has come."

Strength and Bright Hope   MARCH 19

Isaiah 42:1-9 and Matthew 3:13-17

Behold, the former things have come to pass, and new things I now declare.   ISAIAH 42:9A (RSV)

ISAIAH USED THE MEMORY OF GOD'S FAITHFULNESS in the past as a way of reminding His people that He is still active, still working out His divine and gracious plan for them. Israel needed to hear that, because at the time they were living in exile, a captured people.

Many things can happen to us that cause us to "lose control" of our lives. Sometimes older people find themselves no longer able to do things they have enjoyed doing over the years. They may even find themselves "confined" in a place where others determine their schedule of meals, rest time, and so on. Such a condition can make it easy to feel bitter, resentful, even hopeless. But it is not the situation that has the final say as to how we are going to feel inside. We have a choice to make about what we will do with the situation—and that can make all the difference.

Other circumstances that offer difficulty are temporary illnesses or disabilities, loss of loved ones, the breakup of a marriage, the seeming lack of care from those we have depended on for emotional support. Facing these conditions, we have to choose between being controlled by them or seeing God's hand in our lives.

If you are encountering difficulties now, let your memory of past mercies be a cause for thanksgiving. Make a conscious effort to recall the good things that God allowed to come in your life. Thank and praise Him in your heart. Then look around and begin to thank Him for His grace and goodness in the present. He is there. He is giving you grace every moment to face anything He sends your way. Let Him open your eyes to see your way out of any mental or emotional "prison," and let Him lead you to inner joy and peace. Even in the midst of difficulties, He gives His beloved ones peace.

This life is preparing us for eternal life with God. We are a people of hope. The hymn writer says it well: "Strength for today and bright hope for tomorrow." Standing on His faithfulness, ask for those needed gifts: strength and hope. He will not fail you.

The Faith That Overcomes   MARCH 20

I John 5:1-6 and Matthew 28:11-20

And this is the victory that overcomes the world: our faith . . .
I JOHN 5:4B (RSV)

IT IS A TRITE BUT TRUE FACT that the world is passing away. Several years ago, one of our weekly news magazines ran a feature article entitled, "Running Out of Everything" emphasizing the fact that resources of the world are not unlimited—coal, oil, metals, etc.—and that we're going to have to learn how to get along with less, or make do with other things, eventually.

It is said that the English parson, Henry Lyte, looked around his rectory and church yard as day was drawing to a close and penned the words of his immortal hymn, "Abide with Me." They read, in part, "Change and decay in all around I see; O Thou who changest not, abide with me."

The world has a hard time taking this truth and tries to run away from it. Part of the busyness and frantic activity of this generation, with its noise and speed, is an effort to escape this truth: the world is passing away and everything in it. Even the great monuments and buildings of the ancient past show inevitable signs of decay.

But are we locked into this fading age, simply temporary players on the stage of life? John says emphatically, "No!" Earlier in his epistle, he says, "The world passes away, but he who does the will of God will endure forever." There *is* a way of getting free from the bondage of decay and death: our faith. Jesus Christ, whose resurrection we celebrate, has overcome the world and its decay. Death can do no more to Him. And we can believe Him when He tells us that we too will live with Him. We do not have to think and act like people who have no hope for the future. Our future is as sure as God Himself.

When Our Hearts Ask Why   MARCH 21

Psalm 74 and Romans 5:1-5

*O God, why dost Thou cast us off for ever? Why does Thy
anger smoke against the sheep of Thy pasture?*   PSALM 74:1 (RSV)

WHY IS THIS HAPPENING TO ME? We've all asked that question.
Why do the wicked get away with it? Why is such wrong
allowed to go on in this world? Life yields no simple answers.

The psalmist is asking the same kind of question. It involves
the fate of a people, the integrity of the nation of Israel. He felt
that God's people had a right to be delivered and protected.
Instead, there was ruin on every side. "The enemy has destroyed
everything in the sanctuary. Thy foes have roared in the midst of
thy holy place. (verses 3 and 4)

We like to think of ourselves as God's special concern. And
so we are. But we translate that to mean that, because He loves
us, he will spare us any pain. Then life bumps into something like
the situation described in this psalm. None of the religious for-
mulas work any magic. The pain is still there. The enemy is still
roaring in the midst of the holy place (the heart?). Doubt comes
where faith had seemed strong and we cry out, "Why me?"

The psalmist's prayer did not bring immediate deliverance
from the enemy. So, he goes on to rehearse some of the ways in
which God has made himself known to his people. As he does
this, his mood undergoes a change. He continues to pray for
God's intervening help, but the attitude will be one of supplication, not of demand. "Let not the downtrodden be put to
shame; let the poor and needy praise Thy name." (verse 21)

Paul says to the Philippians, "In everything by prayer and
supplication *with thanksgiving* let your requests be made
known to God." (4:6) When we remember to bless the Lord
"for all his benefits" to us, then we are ready to let our requests
be made known to him. Then we can pray for deliverance without demanding to know, "Why?"

"But"   March 22

Acts 10:34-43 and Luke 24:1-12

But on the first day of the week, at early dawn . . .
LUKE 24:1A (RSV)

ALL SEEMED DARK AND HOPELESS THE DAY AFTER Jesus was crucified. To them who loved Him, He was gone forever. Those who had walked with Him, who had learned from Him and had given their all to Him for the previous three years felt lost and friendless. Only days before, they had been filled with vigorous expectation, looking boldly into a bright future with Jesus as their King. Now, despondent and grieved, they wondered what there was to live for. This is what loss and dejection feel like, and anyone who has experienced the death of someone close, knows its numbing coldness.

However, the Gospel does not leave us in that state of defeat. Jesus' death is *not* the end of the story. A wonderful little word exists in the English language which suddenly opens an endless postscript. Listen to Luke: "*But* on the first day of the week, at early dawn . . . " (Luke 24:1) Or listen to Peter, preaching at the house of Cornelius: "They put him to death by hanging him on a tree; *but* God raised him on the third day and made him manifest." (Acts 10:39-40)

It's not a very pretty word, not graceful on the tongue or soothing to the ear, *but* it gets the point across. It takes everything that is moving in one direction, and suddenly stops it, and reverses it. "But" reminds us that not all is said until God finishes the sentence. We should take our lead from Him:

"It's a gloomy day, *but* Christ is my light."

"I feel lonely, *but* Jesus is very present."

"Things seem impossible, *but* nothing is impossible with God."

"I'm afraid of what tomorrow may bring, *but* I can do all things through Christ who strengthens me."

That silly little word becomes a mighty weapon in our hands because it carries the glorious truth of Christianity. God is not defeated; Jesus Christ is not dead; we are not left alone. Times that make us feel that way are sure to come, *but* then we must declare again: "Christ is risen! The Lord is risen, indeed! Alleluia!"

Mine Eyes Have Seen MARCH 23

Isaiah 61:10 and Luke 2:22-40

Lord, now lettest Thou Thy servant depart in peace, according to Thy word; for mine eyes have seen Thy salvation. . . .
LUKE 2:29, 30 (KJV)

MARY AND JOSEPH WERE FULFILLING the requirement of the Law to present the first-born son to the Lord and give an offering. At the Temple they met two remarkable souls—the aged Simeon, whom God had assured would not die until he had seen the Messiah, and the elderly prophetess Anna, who practically lived in the Temple. Seeing the Child Jesus, Simeon knew immediately that God's promise was now fulfilled.

Simeon rejoiced that he had been permitted to see with his own eyes the One whom God had sent to redeem Israel. Prophetically he said the Child was "a light for revelation to the Gentiles and the glory of Thy people Israel." That little Child was destined to alter the course of history forever—and Simeon was permitted to see Him with his own eyes and hold Him in his arms.

Reading that beautiful canticle, we should be encouraged to think of things our eyes have seen. For we, too, have had the privilege of seeing God's promises fulfilled. Some of us have offered anxious prayers for the healing of sick children. One of our children was desperately ill with acute nephritis. During the long night hours of waiting, my heart continually cried out to God for that child, as did his mother, who spent every day at his side. Today he is alive and well, and serves God as a minister of the Gospel. It is just one of many prayers that have been wonderfully answered.

We would do well to recall other things we have seen—"ordinary miracles" we are so apt to take for granted. For when we think of them, gratitude floods our hearts and crowds out any self-pity. Old Simeon could live out his remaining days "in peace" because of God's faithfulness.

Looking back, we see we have not done all the things we wanted to do (or should have done); also we did, thought or felt things we ought not to have done. But that is past, and God's mercy is extended to us as we ask for His forgiveness. And now we are bidden to start fresh again, remembering the things our "eyes have seen."

Preparation and Hope   MARCH 24

Romans 15:4-13 and Matthew 3:1-12

May the God of hope fill you with all joy and peace in believing, so that by the power of the Holy Spirit you may abound in hope. ROM. 15:13 (RSV)

The voice of one crying in the wilderness: Prepare the way of the Lord, make His paths straight. MATT. 3:3A (RSV)

THESE SCRIPTURES ARE TALKING ABOUT "two sides of the same coin." They are reminding us that we are a people of hope, that we do not have to face the future with fear and foreboding. Our God is a God who is preparing wonderful things for those who love Him. Even in this life, which is filled with difficulties and trials for all of us, there is the assurance that we can "abound in hope" by the power of the Holy Spirit.

John the Baptist, on the other hand, came to preach about preparation. He, too, announced a great thing: "The kingdom of heaven is at hand." It was a striking, even startling message that he brought to his people. They were living in virtual slavery under the harsh yoke of Rome, and he said that the rule of God was "at hand." That would mean something good to any faithful heart.

But it was not enough to hear that God was ready to do a good thing, that He was moving in their lives in a new way. They were being called to respond, to prepare. The hope which was being offered was a motive to change, to wake up from their hopelessness and despair.

It is easy to become dragged down by unpleasant circumstances. It is easy to keep looking at all the negative things in life, so we may even forget that God has called us to be people of hope. This is not a "pie in the sky" kind of unrealistic hope, but the belief that the God who made us, the Savior who redeemed us with His precious blood, the Holy Spirit who is the Unseen yet ever-near Companion, will never leave us to face life alone. He is our Hope and our strength. He is our reason for facing today and tomorrow with faith instead of fear.

How to prepare for what God is bringing? Choose to trust, to obey, to love, and to pray, and ask for a grateful heart. That is great preparation and it leads to great hope!

Songs My Mother Taught Me   MARCH 25

Psalm 96 and Matthew 16:13-20

Sing to the Lord, bless His name; tell of His salvation from day to day. PSALM 96:2 (RSV)

IN 1990, I HAD THE PRIVILEGE of visiting St. Petersburg in Russia. One of the most memorable experiences was our visit to the cemetery where more than a million people are buried—victims of the 900-day siege by Hitler's troops during World War II. The people are buried in mass graves, covering a large, carefully tended expanse. Overlooking the graves is an heroic statue of "mother Russia" extending a garland of oak leaves, symbolic of the country's debt of gratitude to the people who refused to surrender to the Nazi forces. At the time we were there, soft music could be heard and the song I remember above all others was the hauntingly beautiful "Songs my mother taught me," by Anton Dvorak.

I felt I wanted to share something about "songs my mother taught me." For I was very blessed to have a mother who loved hymns and often sang them in our hearing as we grew up. I still think of her when I hear a hymn like "How Firm a foundation," or "Amazing Grace." These hymns somehow expressed the spirituality and faith by which she lived and in which she died.

"How Firm a Foundation" bears reading, re-reading, and perhaps even memorizing. "When through the deep waters I call thee to go, the rivers of woe shall not thee overflow." What does that mean in your own life—when you thought that some experience was just about more than you could endure? "When through fiery trials..." I think back and know that my mother taught me more than I realized, just by singing hymns like that and encouraging us to sing them, too. Now they are part of my "mental and spiritual furniture," and I'm grateful for it.

God uses many ways to impart His truth. For some of us, it was mothers and fathers. For others, it was some other person or persons. But no matter how, God has reached all of us with His loving assurance: "The soul that to Jesus hath fled for repose, I will not, I *will not* desert to its foes. That soul, though all hell shall endeavor to shake, I'll never, no never, *no never* forsake!"

AsLong As I Live   MARCH 26

Psalm 146 and Matthew 22:34-46

I will praise the Lord as long as I live; I will sing praises to my
God while I have being.   PSALM 146:2 (RSV)

A DEAR FRIEND LEARNED HER CANCER HAD RETURNED—it
was now far advanced, and the prognosis was not favorable. Someone said to her: "Why don't you make up your mind
to live as long as you're alive?" "That's a very good idea," she
replied. And she did.

There is a temptation to "die" too soon. We may have lost
someone very dear, or we may have had to give up the home we
loved. We may not be able to come and go as we please. The
temptation can be strong to decide that life is over. But if we do
that, we can miss some of God's most important lessons and
richest blessings.

Not all of His blessings seem to be blessings. But God is
love and so is all that comes from His hand. Out of our suffering—or better still, in our suffering—God blesses us in ways we
could never have been blessed without it.

The cross is the greatest example of this mystery that lies at
the core of human life. In this broken world, alienated from its
Creator, suffering is necessary. The cross shows us that God suf-
fers as well as we. God did not choose to create a world where
no suffering could occur, but to make one where we were capable of free choice. Once that free choice was marred by sin, He
took this flawed creation and re-created it through suffering into
something more beautiful and glorious than it would have been
in the first place.

When you are given something to bear—a bitter loss, a pain
that will not go away; when you are asked to walk moment by
moment, not knowing what a day will bring forth—remember,
God is acting in love.

As long as we praise God with our lips, we can depend on
Him to work in our hearts what we cannot work ourselves. We

cannot make ourselves feel brave and strong, but if we keep praising Him for all He has done and is doing, He will give us the courage we need. He has promised never to forsake nor fail those who put their trust in Him.

God's Truthfulness   MARCH 27

Romans 15:4-13 and Matthew 3:1-12

*I tell you that Christ became a servant to the circumcised [His own people] to show God's truthfulness. . . .*ROMANS 15:8A (RSV)

MUCH OF OUR LIFE IS BASED ON TRUST. It would be a miserable world if we did not believe that other people are trustworthy. Yet other people sometimes do let us down, disappoint us, or betray the trust we have put in them.

On the other hand, in our honest moments, we know we have let people down. We may even feel guilty about some incident in which we failed to be what we should have been to someone we loved. I heard a man tell of his failure to respond quickly when his wife's purse was snatched from her and she was knocked into the ditch in the process. His selfish reaction was to wring his hands and ask, "Why is this happening to me?" Yet he loved his wife, and I'm sure was deeply ashamed of his failure later on.

There is one, however, who is ever proving His truthfulness and faithfulness. Why? Because we need a solid, dependable foundation for this life. Life brings pain, the loss of loved ones, unwelcome changes. If we have no foundation of basic trust, we can become bitter, resentful, afraid—twisted caricatures of what we were meant to be. So God proves His truthfulness. Paul says that is why Jesus went among His own people—to fulfill the promises God had made to Abraham centuries before. God remembers, and God wants us to know we can depend on Him.

We have only to think back to see how He has proved His

faithfulness and truthfulness to us. He does not desert us to the problems of life, to face them alone. He is always with us. Even now God is with you, and He wants to bless you, to remind you that He is faithful. He is the God of Truth. One of His greatest promises is this: those who trust in Him will never be confounded. Just as a mother would not fail to answer the cry of her little child, God will not fail to come to us in our need.

His truthfulness invites us to greater faith. As the Psalmist says, "His truth endureth forever."

Glorious in His Faithfulness   MARCH 28

Psalm 125 and James 1:17-27

Every good and perfect gift is from above, coming down from the Father of the heavenly lights, who does not change like shifting shadows. JAMES 1:17 (NIV)

WE KNOW THAT ALL HUMAN LIFE IS CHANGEABLE. Not only do we change physically, but we change inwardly, too. If our changes are maturing ones, if they make our outlook towards others become more merciful and considerate, they are good changes. But if we allow the circumstances that we cannot control to embitter us, then the changes are for worse, not for better. Change *is* taking place. We cannot *not* change.

God, on the other hand, is, as the Scripture tells us, *unchangeable*. He is not unfeeling, but like a good parent, cares what happens to His children. But He cannot change from His nature, which is Love. He cannot be false to Himself, and His promises are based on His absolute trustworthiness.

How grateful we should be that God is unchangeable in His faithfulness to us! He has pledged Himself that He will never leave nor forsake us.

That thought may not occupy our minds when things are going well and we are feeling on top of it all. But when things are *not* going well, and when we are *not* feeling on top of it all it comes into its full importance. I visited one of my brothers a short time before his death. He had lived his life in forgetfulness of God in many ways. Now he was unable to speak and had to communicate by writing. The first thing on his pad to me was, "Please say the 23rd Psalm." God's unchangeable faithfulness meant everything to him at that point.

Think of this when you are feeling down. Think of it when you feel afraid. He is ready, always, to prove His faithfulness.

Nothing Beyond Your Strength   MARCH 29

I Corinthians 10:1-13 and Luke 13:1-9

No temptation has overtaken you that is not common to man. God is faithful, and he will not let you be tempted beyond your strength but with the temptation will also provide the way of escape, that you may be able to endure it. I CORINTHIANS 10:13 (RSV)

OUR TROUBLE IS THAT WE OFTEN DON'T EVEN recognize temptation for what it is. We think of temptation as the impulse to lie, or to have unkind thoughts or say unkind words about others, or the temptation to take something that doesn't belong to us, or to say naughty words—and so on.

Did you ever think about the temptation to try to think ahead and figure out what the future might hold? Did you ever think about the invitation to worry and fret as coming from temptation, and that such thoughts and feelings could be actually resisted and fought against? Did you ever realize that we are all *tempted* to feel sorry for ourselves—perhaps more often than we like to think?

Now such temptations as these are common for all ages, but more common to us as we grow older. Whereas youth faces temptations to the sins of the flesh, we are more apt in later years to be tempted to fear, worry, bitterness, and resentment. If we do not recognize and fight against them, they can lead us to deny the very things by which we have lived many years.

It is a sad picture to see a Christian towards the end of a long pilgrimage, sitting down and feeling sorry for himself or herself because of things that can no longer be. Life was never meant to be a snapshot of the past. A picture of a beautiful village, with a mill pond and dreamy willows, and white clapboard houses and having no breeze stirring even to move leaf or limb, may be a pretty one for a calendar, but life is not like that. If we went to the place where the picture was made, we would see movement. But if we are living day by day as a gift from God, living in the present, rather than wanting what cannot be nor trying to figure out what is lying ahead—we would have much greater peace and patience.

Today's text promises that He is faithful. He is faithful. He is faithful. Keep remembering that great word! And with any trial, any trouble or any temptation to fear, or worry, He is there to show us the way through. What we have to do is to keep in harmonious fellowship with Him *today*. He will take care of tomorrow.

An Invitation and a Command   MARCH 30

Acts 17:22-31 and John 14:15-31

Peace I leave with you, my peace I give unto you; not as the world gives do I give to you. Let not your hearts be troubled, neither let them be afraid.   JOHN 14:27 (RSV)

THESE WORDS OF JESUS, "Let not your heart be troubled," are both an invitation and a command. Jesus knows how easy it is to give in to fear. When we are confronted with bad news, or when we get sick or something bad happens to someone dear to us, our *natural* reaction is fear. We do not know what is going to happen and we have no control over it.

Lacking the ability to control it, we can easily fall into anger, crabbiness, self-pity, even depression. Is there not a better way to react to difficulty for a child of God?

Jesus invites us to look at such things through the eyes of faith, by the help of the Holy Spirit, the Comforter. The secret of the Christian is that there *is* an invisible source of strength and peace in the face of all our needs.

This is more than an invitation, however. It is a command. Perhaps you yourself have given such a command to someone— such as, "Snap out of it! Shape up!" What you were calling for was an inner change of attitude. Your fear and mine, your worry and mine—these do not honor God. We can deal with them by seeing them as they are, confessing them as evidence of our lack of faith and lack of thankfulness for God's past mercies.

"Lord, I am afraid, and I know that this means I am not trusting You as I should. You have always been faithful, and I'm sorry for my lack of faith. Forgive me for not trusting You, and change my heart. I choose to believe that You are working to bring good out of this circumstance [name whatever it is that is making you afraid]. Nothing is greater than Your love and nothing can separate me from it. Amen."

Little Things Mean a Lot   MARCH 31

Psalm 19 and James 3:1-12

Or take ships as an example. Although they are so large and are driven by strong winds, they are steered by a very small rudder wherever the pilot wants to go.   JAMES 3:4 (NIV)

REMEMBER A POPULAR SONG MANY YEARS AGO with the title, "Little Things Mean a Lot?" One friend said she couldn't remember the song, but agreed with its sentiments. Another mentioned "a smile, a touch, a small bouquet." Whatever the songwriter included, it is a positive sentiment worth thinking about.

James was thinking along a little different line when he wrote the inspired words of today's New Testament reading. The real object of his concern was the human tongue, and the damage it can do. It is true that we can inflict "verbal abuse" on others, and real hurt can ensue that may take a long time to get over. Who has not known of harsh words said in anger that broke long-standing relationships? Again little things mean a lot.

So, here we have the two sides, positive and negative, of "little things" that make a difference. On the one hand, since we know how much little things can mean to us, we need to cultivate the habit of passing along these little positive gestures and words of affection to others. My wife gave me a little book earlier this year called *Random Acts of Kindness*. It is a compilation of little incidents in which people have either received or been moved to do something kind for someone with no thought of return. The editors suggest that if such an idea were put into widespread practice, it could change the world. Surely it was such a thought when Jesus said, "If someone asks to borrow your coat, give him your cloak also."

Most of the "little things" we can do will not be long remembered. Yet, think back on your life and the people who have befriended you, or spoken a kind word to you when you felt low. Do not such memories linger to bless you long after they are done?

So, whoever we are, and however limited we may feel ourselves to be, we have James' warning against the negative memories to remind us that kindness leaves a blessing in its wake.

Blessings Remembered

*Praise the Lord, O my soul,
and forget not all his benefits.
He forgives all my sins and
heals all my diseases;
he redeems my life from
the pit and crowns me with
love and compassion. He
satisfies my desires with good
things, so that my youth is
renewed like the eagle's.*

PSALM 103:2-5 (NIV)

"For I Shall Yet Praise Him"

We had been not getting on well that year, either with each other or with the Lord. For me the walk from home to church became my "slough of despond," a place of heaviness of spirit and a battleground—a place to fight (to run though a troop and climb over a wall)—to believe God was who He said He was.

Frequently, though, when I would turn out of the drive onto the road and begin to struggle, a still small voice inside me would say "Something good will happen next May." I kept clinging to that, my only ray of hope.

In May the words we all dread were said aloud: "Gordon, you have cancer—multiple myeloma. We don't know what causes it and we have no cure for it." But now it was May when God had promised a good thing would happen. And so I believed (grace abounds) that Gordon's diagnosis was a good thing.

We began the rounds, doctor's visits, chemotherapy, tests and more tests. As Gordon responded well to medication, he was sent to New England Medical Center and accepted into the bone marrow transplant program there.

And then the time of testing really began. "Testing" is a badly chosen word, for He was not testing us, He was loving us and training us. As the cancer began to grow, the side effects did too—calcium overload, pneumonia, decreased kidney function. The following May was the time set for the bone marrow transplant, but it was delayed over and over again. Someone else needed the place, the calcium overload or his badly functioning kidney could not take the severe treatments. So chemo was stepped up, along with repeated transfusions of blood and other bodily fluids. Gordon fell and cut his leg open right on the bone and, because of his low blood count, it would not heal. He was admitted many times to the hospital.

On one such occasion, Dr. Miller said the transplant would be delayed at least a month for the leg to heal. I cried a good deal of the way home, until a deep assurance came within. "God knows what He is doing," I cried to Betsy who was driving. We laughed, for of course that is true, but for the first time in my life it was a reality; a reality I have not lost—a place to return to in my hardest times.

And so the weeks went by. In December he was so bad that, upon his admission, they decided to get him in the best shape possible and do the bone marrow transplant: it would be the last chance. I moved to Boston; they closed the door to the sterile room and it began.

A new time, a new learning to trust God as I watched the procedure and his pain and suffering and also dealt with my own dislike of confinement, and fears of being alone and in a big city during the worst winter on record.

January 6, 1994, Gordon received the bone marrow— Epiphany—always a special day to me, the day the Gentiles first came to Christ. The cells began to grow. February 5th we came home. He was thin, bald, and weak, but alive.

During this period of time so much love, prayer, and care had been poured out on us that it defies description. When we arrived home, our entire church turned out with signs of welcome. I lay in bed that night thinking about it all, and I told God that it was more love than I could bear. He said, "Oh, it is nothing compared to how much I love you."

And so I know, with a knowing that can't be moved, that God who is Love cannot do anything that is not His love for us or for me. It is another deep place within, a place of unshakable ground, a place that I can go back to when things are "too hard to bear."

Things went well until that day in December when Dr. Miller called: the cancer was back. The final phase of God's love for Gordon, the final healings of the soul had begun. "I am a happy man," he often said.

My walks through my own personal "slough of despond" returned as I struggled to continue to believe in God's perfect love for me and His perfect will for Gordon. "I have brought you this far," He would say. "Will you go another step with Me?" "Yes, Lord, for I have no other way to go but with You." Gordon died in May and we buried him with lilacs.

And if it was God's perfect will and perfect love that Gordon should die—and I know this is true—then it is of His love that I should learn to live without a husband.

The heaviness is often there as I walk to church, so I rehearse again the truth I know: God is love and can do nothing that is not love. He is Lord of my life and He has every right to take my husband. I am happy for Gordon. And I say to myself, "Why art thou cast down, O my soul, and why art thou so disquieted within me? Hope thou in God: for I shall yet praise Him." (Psalm 42:5 KJV)

This is my best Scripture—I carry it around in my pocket for the days that are just "too hard": "For I know the plans I have for you, declares the Lord, plans to prosper you and not to harm you, plans to give you hope and a future." (Jeremiah 29:11 NIV)

Lyn Clark

That Little Word "If" APRIL 1

Philippians 2:1-13 and Matthew 21:28-32

If there is any encouragement in Christ, any incentive of love,
any participation in the Spirit, any affection and sympathy,
complete my joy. . . . PHILIPPIANS 2:1 (RSV)

"IF THOU WILT," SAID THE LEPER TO JESUS, "Thou canst make me clean." Jesus answered, "I will! Be clean!" Immediately the man was healed. "If I only touch the hem of His garment, I shall be made well," said the woman who had suffered from an internal hemorrhage for twelve years. She touched the hem of His garment, and was made well. "If any man would come after me," said Jesus, "let him take up his cross daily and follow me." *If.*

And now Paul uses that little word. He urges us to claim our heritage in Christ, appealing to all we have experienced in our walk with God—the motivating love of God within, the inner joy and activity of the Holy Spirit, the affection we feel for our loved ones and friends. If any of these things are real, he says, "You can complete my joy" by being in full accord with one another. He wanted no ill will or differences among the little Christian groups. Surrounded by outward enemies, they needed the strength and help they could give one another.

Joy comes when we let it in. Just as the morning light dispels the shadows and fears of the night, joy comes in to dispel dark fears and self-pitying thoughts. The eighteenth-century English hymn writer William Cowper was afflicted with recurring bouts of depression. Yet his hymns still ring true to us today. In one of them he says:

Sometimes a light surprises
The Christian as he sings;
It is the Lord who rises
With healing in His wings:
When comforts are declining,

He grants the soul again
A season of clear shining,
To cheer it after rain.

Our joy, our cheer, is tied in with our awareness of Jesus
and His love for us. Before He left His disciples, He said, "You
have sorrow now, but I will see you again and your hearts will
rejoice, and no one will take your joy from you." (John 16:22)
That's a great word of promise. No matter what our outward
situation, there is a secret joy which nothing can take from us.
Let us claim that promise today.

Peace with God   APRIL 2

Exodus 17:1-7 and Romans 5:1-11

*Therefore, since we are justified by faith, we have peace with
God through our Lord Jesus Christ.*   ROMANS 5:1 (RSV)

SOMEONE DID SOME RESEARCH YEARS AGO and concluded
that there was no sustained period throughout recorded history when there was not war *somewhere* on this planet. We are
not a peaceful race.

One of the Bible's greatest words is "peace." When the
angels appeared to the shepherds to announce the birth of
Jesus, they spoke of "peace on earth among men of goodwill."
Paul says of Jesus, "He came and preached peace to you who
were afar off and peace to those who were near." (Eph. 2:17
NIV) In another place he says of Jesus, "He is our peace." It is
one of the great longings of the human heart—to have peace.

But we are not talking about peace between nations, or
even between people. We are talking about the deeper, more
fundamental peace we all need. Whether we are busy, active people, trying to keep up with a thousand demands, or "retired"
and more limited in our activities, we need an inner peace. The
root of that peace must be the peace with God which Paul refers

to here. Unless we have that peace, we have no anchor, no stability in the midst of trouble. But if we have peace there, we can stand in the storms of life, knowing that all is well within.

How do we attain it? By the most simple act of trust in what God has done for us in Jesus Christ. By setting aside all our intellectual doubts, and going to Him with our needs, our sins, our failures, and our hopes. By allowing Him to carry the burden of our care in His heart. That faith is so precious to God that He uses it as the ground to settle peace within us. Our faith is built on the goodness and mercy of God who brings peace to His people. If you have need of that peace in your heart, please take the opportunity to go to Jesus in faith, and accept His gift of love to you. His will for you is peace.

Blessed With Peace APRIL 3

Psalm 29

The Lord will give strength unto His people; the Lord will bless His people with peace. PSALM 29:11 (KJV)

IN THIS 29TH PSALM, THE WRITER GIVES US a poetic picture of the majesty of God, seen in the thunder, wind and lightning of a great storm. I can remember watching such storms as a child and feeling my own littleness and helplessness before them.

Storms are pictures of life, with its upheavals, dangers—its "shakings." We have all passed through storms of different kinds. What our text is saying to us is that God "sits above the storms of life": "The Lord sits upon the flood; yea, the Lord sitteth King for ever." (verse 10) There are no circumstances that are beyond His care, His concern and His power. He is present *in* every storm of life, the Ruler of its winds and waves.

I am glad we have that assurance, because some of the storms are frightening enough to dismay the bravest among us if we do not know that God is in charge. A sudden turn of illness, the breaking of some tragic news about someone we love—these things can throw us into confusion and shake us to the very foundations. Then we need to remember that the God of the Storm is with us, and He has promised to give us strength for every need. If we do not find that strength at once, we must keep on asking earnestly for it until it comes, and come it surely will!

But the Lord Stood by Me   APRIL 4

II Timothy 4:6-8, 16-18 and Luke 18:9-14

At my first defense no one took my part; all deserted me . . .
But the Lord stood by me and gave me strength . . .
II TIMOTHY 4:16A, 17 (RSV)

THIS LETTER TO YOUNG TIMOTHY is one of the most moving passages we have from the hand of this aging apostle. He is obviously nearing the end of his life, and his needs are plain. "When you come, bring the cloak I left with Carpus at Troas." He was feeling the chill of his Roman prison. "Also the books, and above all the parchments." He needed encouragement and challenge from the words of others.

How like us! Young or old, we need both physical and spiritual help along the way, and it is the wise person who learns to acknowledge and ask for it.

Paul's testimony, after his ordeal of being tried (apparently before the Roman imperial court) was this: although no human aid was forthcoming, God was still faithful. That is such an important truth that we can hardly overemphasize it. For the time comes in every one of our lives when human help is not available. Sometimes, as in the case of Paul, it is the faithlessness of those on whom we have depended. They simply leave us "in the lurch" at the critical moment.

But there are other circumstances in which our loved ones

simply cannot go beyond a certain point—regardless of their loyalty and concern for us. Human aid will not carry us all the way.

Here is where the aging apostle has something to say to us: "But the Lord stood by me." That was his testimony of God's unfailing faithfulness. And on that he built his last great affirmation, possibly the last word we have from his inspired pen: "The Lord *will* rescue me from every evil and save me for His heavenly kingdom." (verse 18) On the basis of God's past faithfulness, Paul counted on His help in anything that might lie ahead. So can we.

Whence Cometh My Help? APRIL 5

Psalm 121 and James 1:12-16

I lift up my eyes to the hills—where does my help come from?
My help comes from the Lord, the Maker of heaven and earth.
PSALM 121:1, 2 (NIV)

THIS MIGHT BE CALLED THE "SLEEPLESS PSALM." We are assured that He who watches over us will not slumber nor sleep.

I read a story years ago about a certain bishop who fretted and worried about many things. As you may know, such worries can make for a long night! And at some point, the bishop inwardly heard the voice of the Lord saying softly, "My son, you may go to sleep; I'll stay awake."

It seems that no matter how old we get, there is a little child somewhere inside us that that needs comfort at times. Perhaps it is especially true as we get older and are more aware of our own frailty and mortality. If we have cultivated a relationship with our heavenly Father that is close and intimate, it stands us in good stead. If we have been careless, it may take more effort to grasp the fullness of what the psalmist says here: "My help comes from the Lord, the Maker of heaven and earth." It would not be an exaggeration to say that for most of us, our concept of God is too small. We are like the woman on the airplane who wouldn't sit back comfortably because she was afraid the airplane wouldn't hold her up. We are "on board" with God. We say we believe in Him, and most, if not all, of you who read these words have committed yourselves to Jesus Christ as your personal Lord and Savior. Yet in spite of that, our trust is weak; our faith is imperfect.

I suppose the only way we learn to embrace and accept the psalmist's assurance is by going through the dark valleys, struggling through nights when we feel alone, enduring times when God seems absent or far away. And yet, He doesn't let us down. Time after time He proves His love, and with a little stronger, more faith-filled voice we can say,

"My help comes from the *Lord, the Maker of Heaven and Earth*," and mean it.

Where Are the Nine? APRIL 6

II Timothy 2:8-15 and Luke 17:11-19

Then said Jesus, "Were not ten cleansed? Where are the nine? Was no one found to return and give praise to God except this foreigner? LUKE 17:17, 18 (RSV)

HOW EASY IT IS TO JUDGE THESE UNFORTUNATE LEPERS, who got so excited about their new-found blessing that they greedily ran on their way to enjoy it, and forgot to return thanks and praise to the One who had made it possible!

Could that question apply to us? Were there not ten blessings? Where are the thanks and praise for the nine you forgot about as soon as you had enjoyed them?

During World War II, I was stationed in the Philippines and used to attend a little unofficial chapel that some Christians had erected, using an old tent. On Saturday night a whole truckload of us would join with others, black and white, to sing hymns and hear a message by a lay preacher. One prayer I remember quite vividly. "Lord, our past mercies are all used up. We are in need of new ones." From time to time I think about that: past mercies are all used up. Do I daily remember to give thanks for those that are coming from God, fresh as the morning dew? The answer is, No. Not always. Sometimes I greedily devour them, like these nine lepers, and forget to turn and give thanks.

God is very patient with us. Jesus did not say, "Well, since they didn't even say thank you we'll just let the leprosy come back." Thank God, He is not like that. We human beings sometimes act that way when people don't appreciate what we've given them or done for them. We may say, "Well if that's the way they're going to act, it will be a cold day in July before I do something nice for them again."

And all the while, we are forgetting how many times we forgot to give thanks and praise to God. Where are the nine? How many blessings can you name that your loving heavenly Father has poured upon you in the past week? It will be worth your while to name them, and to thank Him for them.

When All Seems Hopeless   APRIL 7

Genesis 17:1-7, 15-16 and Romans 4:16-25

In hope he [Abraham] believed against hope, that he should become the father of many nations; as he had been told, "So shall your descendants be."   ROMANS 4:18 (RSV)

WE ALL KNOW THE STORY OF ABRAHAM, and how God promised a son to him and Sarah when she was well "past the age of childbearing." Paul emphasizes that Abraham's faith, his trust in what seemed an absolute impossibility, was what God "reckoned to him as righteousness."

Do you face some situation in your life at this moment that

seems hopeless? Is there some circumstance that defies human solution, and from a natural standpoint could be a subject of despair? If so, today's Scriptures may be a special word of encouragement for you.

Paul tells us to make our supplications *with thanksgiving.* Don't forget that God has invited us to ask for the impossible, and that He can do what we cannot do!

God gave Abraham His amazing promise *in his helplessness.* You can see what a door of hope is opened as this story unfolds. When all seems hopeless, we can remember that God is still God, that He is still on His throne, and that He bids us to come with all our need. Abraham trusted God to do what He had promised. God has promised you and me many, many great things: that He will be with us and supply that inner need we cannot muster by ourselves. "In hope, he believed against hope." What a difference that can make! And we'll never know until we try!

Lest We Forget   APRIL 8

Deuteronomy 4:1-9 and Mark 7:1-8, 14-23

Only take heed, and keep your soul diligently, lest you forget
the things which your eyes have seen, and lest they depart
from your heart. . . .   DEUT 4:9A (RSV)

A S I GET OLDER, my well-developed capacity for forgetting things seems to grow even greater. It is *so* easy to forget where I left my car keys, or some letter I meant to save, or if I have taken a certain pill.

There is another thing, I find, that it is easy to forget. It is easy to forget past blessings. Because of this tendency, several years ago I started keeping a "Blessing Book" to record my thanksgivings to God for the blessings—some large and some small, but all blessings—so I should not forget them.

Moses was very concerned that Israel remember what had happened during his lifetime. They had literally been delivered from grinding slavery into the dignity, nobility, and opportunity of being a free people under God. Succeeding generations could easily take that for granted, and it was important for them to remember where they had come from. And so it is with us. Every one of us has been led along a path. It is not always a smooth path, and may not always have been filled with joy. But God was there, and His hand was leading us. Eyes of faith can look back and see His mercies over all our way.

There is a significant phrase here in this verse from Deuteronomy. They were to remember these things "lest they depart from your heart." Israel faced the possibility of losing the very faith that had sustained them through those long wilderness years.

Sickness, disability, confinement to home or a nursing home, the natural limitations of age—these can try our faith. Unless we keep watch, unless we *remember*, it is easy to fall into despair and bitterness. But we can think of it this way: God sees where we are, and how much we have grown inwardly in our relationship with Him. And He lovingly allows the circumstance to test the mettle of our commitment. He promises never to leave nor forsake us, but we, on our part, must choose not to leave nor forsake Him—even when the path is rough and steep.

Remembering past blessings is one way of bringing joy and cheer into present circumstances. On the basis of them we can lift up our hearts, believing that He is still faithful to carry us through.

A New Look at Sacrifice   APRIL 9

Romans 12:1-8 and Matthew 16:21-27

I beseech you therefore, brethren, by the mercies of God, that ye present your bodies a living sacrifice, holy and acceptable unto God, which is your reasonable service. Romans 12:1 (kjv)

ISRAEL OF OLD BROUGHT THEIR ANIMALS to be offered on the altar to the Lord. The idea behind it was that the sacrifice somehow made reparation for the offense of sin which brought separation from God.

What Paul is saying when he counsels us to present our bodies as "a living sacrifice" is not that we must appease God's anger or make up for something. God has already dealt with our sins on the cross, where His beloved Son, in our place, made "a full, perfect and sufficient sacrifice for the sins of the whole world." "For God so loved the world that He *gave* His only begotten Son. . ." (John 3:16)

Because God in His love has provided everything we need to have abundant life here and in all eternity, we can do nothing less than respond with *all* we are and can be. Paul means our total self should be presented to God as a living offering.

Practically speaking, what is a living sacrifice? Our text describes this living sacrifice as "your reasonable service" (kjv) or as "your spiritual worship" (rsv). It means the inner life, the heart, our "lifestyle," the way we think and act. If the inner life is given to God, the outward life will show it.

A living sacrifice means putting God's will ahead of our own. Jesus Himself prayed, "Nevertheless, not what I will, but as Thou wilt." And He taught us in the Lord's Prayer, "Thy will be done on earth as it is in heaven." It is not always easy to bend our wills to His, but He does ask us to submit our dreams, plans, and ambitions to His greater will, promising us "by the mercies of God" that His way is best. Right in the midst of making a sacrifice, we can have abundant life.

Forget Not! APRIL 10

Psalm 103 and John 20:10-31

Bless the Lord, O my soul, and forget not all His benefits, who
forgives all your iniquity, who heals all your diseases, who
redeems your life from the pit . . ., who satisfies you with good
as long as you live, so that your youth is renewed like the eagle's.
PSALM 103:2-5 (RSV)

HERE WE HAVE A CATALOG OF HIS ONGOING MERCIES! Forget not! For we are forgetful people.

He forgives. "He forgives all your iniquities." That includes those hidden sins of thought and feeling that we have confessed to no one. We can lay bare these wounds of our souls and receive forgiveness and healing.

He heals. He is the Great Physician. Healing is promised and healing is sure. Here we enter into a mystery, because for some people the healing does not come in the form we ask or expect. So we know His unqualified promise to heal means that healing of the inner person sometimes takes priority over the temporary healing of the body.

He redeems. The picture here is being rescued from the "bottomless pit." There are many "bottomless pits" in this life. These pits are a result of bad choices, self-pity, jealousies, and dark thoughts. But our Lord Jesus, our Redeemer, has entered our world to bring us out of these miry pits and to set our feet on the solid Rock.

He satisfies. The sad thing about most of us is that we do not allow this to happen. We still seek our satisfaction from things that are passing away. We long for place and position, power and prestige. We clutter our life with possessions that neither satisfy nor make us happy. Still we do not give up our belief that life consists "in the abundance of the things that we possess." And so we lack the satisfaction this Psalm promises.

Bless the Lord, O my soul, and forget not all His benefits!

I Believe That I Shall See   APRIL 11

Psalm 27 and Luke 13: 31-35

*I believe that I shall see the goodness of the Lord in the land of
the living! Wait for the Lord; be strong, and let your heart take
courage; yea, wait for the Lord!*   PSALM 27:13, 14 (RSV)

I HAVE BEEN TALKING WITH A FRIEND who is going through a
hard time. Life has become shadowy for him. He has a hard
time thinking positively about his life, and seems to be concen-
trating on all the negative elements in it. I am urging him to
battle the negative thoughts that rise up and try to control his
feelings. It is not something anyone can do for him. He has to
struggle with the inner accusations that others have let him
down and reject the thoughts that life is not treating him fairly.

The psalmist here talks about his enemies. "Evil doers, slan-
derers, adversaries and foes; false witnesses and men who
breathe out violence." At this point the psalmist could spend
much time and energy rehearsing all the misfortunes and all the
negative things he could think of. Instead, he says, "I believe
that I shall see the goodness of the Lord in the land of the living."
It was a choice, and he made the right one.

There have been times in all our lives, I suspect, when we
made the wrong choice, and did not believe we would see the
goodness of the Lord. We were "down and out" and we felt *overwhelmed* with misfortune. But light came again into our darkness. Hope renewed. Faith revived, and we were able to go on.
One of the ways of battling the darkness of our feelings when
things are hard for us is deliberately to *praise* God for his goodness. We may feel as dead as doornails, and our words may seem
to go nowhere. But our praise is heard, and somewhere, somehow, light begins to break in. Even when I cannot see it now, by
faith I can say, "I believe that I shall see the goodness of the Lord
in the land of the living." His light—the light of love, faith, hope-
and peace—is stronger than the negative forces that would weigh
us down. That I believe—for it has been true for me!

Learning through Suffering APRIL 12

Jeremiah 31:7-9 and Mark 10:35-45

*Jesus said, ". . . Are you able to drink the cup that I drink, or to
be baptized with the baptism with which I am baptized?
And they said to Him, "We are able."* MARK 10:38-39 (RSV)

THE BOOK OF HEBREWS SAYS that Jesus Himself, the very Son
of God, "was perfected and learned obedience through what
He suffered." He did not *seek* suffering, but when it came, he
accepted it. He allowed it to mature and change Him. It is a holy
mystery that we meet here, but one we do well to think about.
The holy, perfect Son of God was matured and "perfected"
through His suffering. The question we need to ask is this: What
about the things we are called to endure and suffer? Surely God
must have a loving purpose in and through them.

A friend of mine some time ago was ordered to take a three-
week stay "flat on his back" in bed. The pain he experienced at
the beginning was extreme. But he said to me, "It has been one
of the greatest blessings of my life, because of what God is
showing and teaching me. I would never have let it happen if
God had not allowed this to come upon me." He was learning
through his suffering.

We all go through different kinds of pains, hardships, disappointments, disabilities, and deprivations at various points in
our lives. We can choose to let those experiences mature us
inside, as Jesus did, or we can waste them in self-pity, anger,
and resentment. Jesus learned what obedience is and what it
sometimes costs. And because He experienced that, He can be
a "very present help in trouble" for us. He knows what it feels
like!

What do you do with your suffering? Waste it, or use it?
God wants to bless you in and through it. The choice is yours.

A Time for Every Matter under Heaven   APRIL 13

Ecclesiastes 3:1-13 and Colossians 3:12-17

For everything there is a season, and a time for every matter under heaven. . . God has made everything beautiful in its time; also He has put eternity into man's mind. . . ECC. 3:1, 11 (RSV)

WHAT A THOUGHT WITH WHICH TO LOOK at the future. It is a time of grace; a time of promise; a time in which God's faithfulness will be proved over and over for you and me.

Do we see tomorrow with fear, or with hope? With anxiety about what it may hold, or with thanksgiving for *today*? The way we will experience our tomorrows will depend very much on the attitude with which we receive them.

Life is fraught with uncertainties. God must have meant it that way, or it would be different. Aren't you glad, when you really think about it, that you cannot tell what the future holds? There had to be love and mercy behind His wise design that we could *remember* the past (and learn from it) and we could *trust* Him for the future as it unfolds. Worry is a way of discounting God's past mercies. It is a way of rejecting His present help. We borrow needless trouble when we allow ourselves to project our thoughts into what "might be," or "might happen."

As we read over the list of things the writer of Ecclesiastes mentions—a time to be born, a time to die, etc., it reminds us that things do have a season, a timeliness about them. Fruit ripens—it does not come full-blown from the bud and flower. And life ripens, too, if we cooperate with God in the process.

It is always a good time to remember what He has done in the past—many of His mercies have been forgotten in the ongoing pace of life. If life is a little slower now for you, it is time to reflect, recall, and remember: He has made everything beautiful *in its time*. Let gratitude rise up like a wellspring in your heart.

Yes, He has led and He is leading. Rejoice and take hope in that. He will not—He *cannot* fail!

Recounting His Steadfast Love APRIL 14

Isaiah 63:7-9 and Hebrews 2:10-18

I will recount the steadfast love of the Lord, the praises of the Lord, according to all that the Lord has granted us and the great goodness to the house of Israel which He has granted them according to His mercy. ISAIAH 63:7 (RSV)

THERE IS NO BETTER TIME TO "RECOUNT the steadfast love of the Lord" than today. Whatever the past may have held for you in terms of joy or sorrow, pain or loss, success or failure, it has been blessed by the Lord's mercy. I have absolutely no doubt of that, because the God we know and serve is ever merciful to His children.

We are all tempted at times to get "down in the dumps." It may be bad indigestion. It may be the temperature of the room, or the fact that someone didn't come to see us as we had hoped or expected. It can be a thousand and one things that get us down, and then we're tempted to forget "the steadfast love of the Lord."

The cure for that is to recount. "Count your many blessings, name them one by one, and it will surprise you what the Lord has done." God deserves a thankful people. He deserves our praise.

An unthankful heart is a heavy burden to drag into the future. I believe God wants to remove from our back the heavy burdens of an ungrateful heart along with anxiety about the future. The best preparation I know for the future is to recount the goodness and mercy of the Lord in the past.

The best way I know to handle those inevitable disappointments we all experience is to say "God knows what He is doing." And, at this stage in my life, I would like to add, "And He does all things well."

The Gentleness of God APRIL 15

Isaiah 40:1-11 and Mark 1:1-8

He will feed His flock like a shepherd, He will gather the lambs
in His arms, . . . and gently lead those that are with young.
ISAIAH 40:11 (RSV)

THE CHURCH HAS CALLED THE CREATOR "ALMIGHTY GOD."
Since earliest time, it has been a comfort to remember, especially in times of great need, that our God is indeed almighty. When it looks as though evil men or strange accidents seem to be "in charge," it is good to remember that our trust has been placed in the One who made all things, and that "He's got the whole world in His hands." When children are afraid, they run instinctively to the protection of a parent's reassurance. When we face situations that make us afraid, do we not seek refuge in God's almighty strength?

But power alone does not fill our need. In fact, power can be a very frightening thing. If we believed in a God who was simply almighty, we might cringe before Him, but we would hardly love Him! Our God, the Father of our Lord Jesus Christ, is depicted in the Bible as tender as a mother caring for her child. Strength is wedded to gentleness.

So He blesses us with the revelation of His real character with this invitation: "Come unto me, all ye that labor and are heavy-laden, and I will give you rest. Take my yoke upon you and learn of me. For I am gentle and lowly in heart, and you will find rest for your souls." (Matthew 11:28, 29)

One of the greatest joys I have as a minister of Christ is to be able to share this good news with people: Almighty God is a God of love and gentleness. He desires our good. He works with every situation in life for good. "All things work for good to those who love Him, to those who are called according to His purpose." He never lays on us more than we can bear, and He always helps us bear whatever load we have. And that, my dear friend, is truly good news!

Our Need for Endurance   APRIL 16

Hebrews 10:32-39 and Mark 13:14-23

Therefore do not throw away your confidence, which has a
great reward. For you have need of endurance, so that you may
do the will of God and receive what is promised.
HEBREW 10:35-36 (RSV)

NOT EVERYONE WHO STARTS IN A RACE WINS. It is the finishing, not the starting that counts. And life can be compared in many ways to a race. It has its enthusiastic starts, its uphills and downs, its hindrances and distractions, its weariness and its refreshments. But the object of the race is its goal—the finishing.

The Christian life is a peculiar kind of race. It's one in which we can all win the crown. It's not the speediness but the steadiness that makes the difference. The people to whom this text was directed were having a difficult time. Some were being persecuted, while others were simply being persuaded that they weren't believing in the truth. The devil doesn't mind what tactic he uses, so long as it discourages us in our race. Sometimes he uses outright persecution.

More often, however, it is the "little foxes that destroy the vine." By that I mean little discouragements and disappointments that just get us down and dim our faith. We may not be tempted to an outright denial, but in fact, when we let our attitude and feelings get so negative, we are denying the great hope and truth which we have been given. And so we need to be reminded that no matter what, we are called to endurance. "Do not throw away your confidence." The clouds pass, the sun reappears, and we know again that there is light on our path. Jesus Christ, the same yesterday, today and forever, is still on His throne. And we can enthrone Him by enduring today's challenges with confidence and faith.

Keeping Our Priorities Straight APRIL 17

Galatians 6:14-18 and Luke 10:1-20

*Nevertheless do not rejoice in this, that the spirits are subject to
you; but rejoice that your names are written in heaven.*
LUKE 10:20 (RSV)

THE DISCIPLES OF JESUS HAD SEEN His mighty works, witnessed miraculous healings, and seen demon-possessed
people freed from their afflictions. Now to their great joy, they
were able to see similar healings and deliverances in answer to
their own prayers and ministry.

But Jesus is concerned that they should keep their priorities
straight. Yes, it was wonderful that they could be used to help
people in this way. But life here is still a life of mortality. Jesus'
mission for them and for all whom they would reach was far
greater than bringing physical or emotional relief. It was to call
them to eternal life and prepare them for a life that would never
end.

This is as important for us as it was for them. We all have
our own concerns about our physical and emotional problems.
We should be very grateful for the many advances in science
that God has allowed for our good and comfort. A dear friend
of mine had to take medication for a certain stubborn physical
condition. At first she resented the medicine very much. But
God taught her instead to bless the medicine and everyone connected with its development and manufacture—each time she
had to swallow a pill. It changed her whole attitude toward it,
she said. For these things really are blessings from the Lord, and
we should be grateful for them.

But—we still need to keep eternity in view! Our eternal home
is not here—but with God. The old Gospel song asks the question,
"Is my name written there?" Have we turned over our future to
our Savior, saying, "Lord, I give myself to You and I receive You
for my Savior and my Lord"? He says that we will not be disappointed if we put our trust in Christ—and we can believe that!

We are meant to live with God through all eternity. Even the longest life here is but a brief span. Let's make sure we keep our priorities straight, and live in the peace and assurance that, as the hymn says, "I am His and He is mine for ever."

He Will Perform It   APRIL 18

Philippians 1:3-11 and Luke 1:68-79

Being confident of this very thing, that He which hath began a good work in you will perform it until the day of Jesus Christ.
PHILIPPIANS 1:6 (KJV)

IT IS A SURPRISING THOUGHT TO MANY PEOPLE that God has begun "a good work" in them. They may not have thought of themselves as a "work of God," and had little or no idea that He is shaping, molding, sculpting them after His own pattern. But that is exactly what the apostle is saying here, and it is a clue to understanding what is happening to us, if we have eyes to see.

It means, first of all, that God is about a permanent and important business with you. His heart and His eye are fixed on you and on what He is doing with you. He looks at us through the lens of His own creative purpose and His redemptive love, and says, in effect, "I am going to make something beautiful out of this soul." And He asks us to cooperate with Him in that process and to trust what is really going on.

Second, it means that the events and circumstances of our lives are all part of this process. And that's the rub for many of us. We look at disappointments, at failures, at loss of loved ones, at illness or disability as occasions for self-pity, grief, perhaps anger, despair, and bitterness. But the reality is that God is at work in every one of these things to complete His work in us. We cannot see how it is going to work, for we are called to walk by faith. But by His goodness we can believe and affirm that He will continue until the work is finished in us.

We are invited to take a new view of our lives and everything in them. We are invited to see them through the lens of the unshakable and limitless love of God. He has purposed to make something beautiful out of our souls.

The Lord Will Fulfill His Purpose   APRIL 19

Psalm 138 and Luke 11:1-13

The Lord will fulfill His purpose for me; Thy steadfast love,
O Lord, endures for ever.   PSALM 138:8 (RSV)

IN THIS SCRIPTURE WE HAVE ASSURANCE of something very, very important to our peace of mind. God will not abandon the work He has begun in us. As the popular saying goes, "We aren't finished yet."

Why is this important? It is important because we get discouraged with ourselves or our circumstances. Our negative view of things can weaken our faith. In that state, we may begin to lose hope, become bitter, simply trying to endure and wait life out to the end. That is no way for any child of God to think or feel.

The psalmist who wrote today's text must have been feeling discouraged, for his last words are, "Do not forsake the work of Thy hands." That little line tells me that this whole psalm is an exercise in faith, a kind of shining light thrown against some dark circumstance. You and I can exercise that same kind of bold faith. What is the dark circumstance? Is it sickness? Is it bodily weakness? Is it fear of the unknown future? Is it the loss of someone you loved very much? Is it the loss of control over your own life? These can be dark things, and can make us bitter if we choose to let them. But they can be the very place where we assert the goodness and mercy of God. We can, as the psalmist did, go over in our minds the many times God has come to our assistance. We can recount the blessings He has poured on us, and we can remember, too, those times when we sensed that God does indeed love us.

I find great comfort and strength in remembering that God is still at work in my soul. If He hasn't given up on us, we certainly cannot afford to give up on ourselves. God is for you. Who can be against you?

Seek the Things Above APRIL 20

Colossians 3:1-11 and Luke 24:46-53

If then you have been raised with Christ, seek the things that are above, where Christ is seated at the right hand of God. Set your mind on things that are above. . . . COLOSSIANS 3:1, 2A (RSV)

MANY OF US GET SO CLUTTERED with our little earthly cares that we forget the grand realities of our spiritual heritage. We are children of God! We have been raised to new life with Jesus, who lives forever. At the very longest, our life is but a handbreadth when measured against eternity.

Paul reminds these believers at Colossae how foolish it is to get bogged down with worldy cares when their true life was hidden with Christ in God. We are bidden to let our hearts follow Jesus to His Father's home. We can cultivate that by giving more attention to inward prayer and conversation with Him. We do not need to say fancy prayers or think deep thoughts. All we have to do is let our minds and ears dwell on Him: to talk with Him as with a dear friend, letting Him know how we are feeling and what we are thinking.

Life for all of us is a fleeting thing. Jesus knew the value of using the present moment. You and I need to learn the same value, otherwise we will keep postponing the things we mean to do, and never get around to doing them.

Ask yourself these questions about seeking the things above: (1) What am I holding on to that God would have me let go of? (2) Do I need to tell someone how much I love them, or to thank them for kindnesses done? (3) For whom do I need to pray today? (4) Where am I being petty, mean or selfish?

God will show you what He wants you to see; then your mind can be set more and more on things above.

From God's Hand   APRIL 21

I John 3:18-24 and John 10:11-18

I am the good Shepherd, and know my sheep, and am known of mine. JOHN 10:14 (KJV)

WHAT CAN ONE SAY ABOUT THE GOOD SHEPHERD that has not already been said? And yet, what makes our relationship with Him too valuable for words is contained in this little text: He knows us by name and *we* are beginning to recognize Him.

I say "beginning to recognize Him," because we have often mistaken His voice and the outstretched Hand which comes near to us in the circumstances of our lives. Something happens to us that we do not like. It may be something as serious as an illness, the death of someone we love, or some tragedy. Inside we react in anger, in grief, in fear. And so we do not look for His Hand, and do not listen for His Voice *in the situation.*

Someone gave me a little leaflet recently that moved me very deeply. Here, in part, is what the author said:

> My child, I have a message for you today; let me whisper it in your ear, that it may gild with glory any storm clouds which may arise, and smooth the rough places upon which you have to tread.
>
> It is short—only five words—but let them sink into your inmost soul; use them as a pillow upon which to rest your weary head: *This thing is from Me.*

These are some of the things that may come from God's hand: temptations, money difficulties, difficult circumstances, sorrow, disappointment in friends, upsets in plans, being laid aside and unable to be in active service. And through all of them, we're reminded, God is at work, *allowing* these things for our greater good, keeping watch always, always seeking to teach and train us in godliness and drawing us nearer to Himself.

Our choice comes in the way we react. Do we believe that we are "the people of His pasture and the sheep of His hand?" Are we children of the Good Shepherd, and do we expect to belong to Him for ever and ever? Then we can trust His goodness today—no matter what! We can know that He has not abandoned us to fend for ourselves. He cares. For He knows you, just where you are. And He cares.

God Meant it for Good APRIL 22

Genesis 45:3-15; 50:20 and Luke 6:27-38

As for you, you meant evil against me, but God meant it for good. GENESIS 50:20A (RSV)

JOSEPH HAD EVERY REASON TO HARBOR HATRED against his brothers. They had done him a grave injustice, selling him into the living death of slavery.

Joseph suffered immensely as a result of the sin of his brothers against him. Stripped of the protection and care of his father and carried to a strange land, he ended up being falsely accused of a crime and thrown into prison.

From this encounter with his brothers it is clear that Joseph had not wasted the experience of the years, but had come to see God's hand in his life. We are all called to do the same. We could all cite things that have been done to us that were wrong—unloving things from people, or their neglect of us. If we hold onto such things, we miss the very blessing God intends for us.

It is a spiritual principle that God means everything in our lives for good. That includes the bad as well as the good. We are not let loose in an out-of-control world gone amuck. God is still able to fashion out of tragedy, wrong, sin, and evil, something which will eventuate in good.

It was not only to Joseph's personal credit that he was able to forgive his brothers the evil they had done. It was to the saving of his inner life, because holding on to the hatred would have kept him from receiving what God had for him in Egypt. Only a man free of bitterness could receive the divine guidance Joseph had, which saved Egypt and his own family in the famine that lay ahead. What a beautiful picture of how God takes the worst and turns it for the best!

Our Lord Jesus, when they were nailing Him to the cross, prayed, "Father, forgive them, for they know not what they do." It was the release of a forgiving spirit, and was meant to be emulated by everyone of us who claim to believe in Him. Holding on to bitterness can keep us from seeing the miracle: "You meant evil against me, but God meant it for good." And saying that, we can be free to see and receive the good.

Your Father Knows   APRIL 23

Jeremiah 23:23-29 and Luke 12:29-56

And do not seek what you are to eat and what you are to drink, nor be of anxious mind. For all the nations of the world seek these things, and your Father knows that you need them.
LUKE 12:29, 30 (RSV)

IT'S EASY FOR ME TO BE DISCONTENTED if the circumstances of my life don't line up just right. If the day has duties which I find irksome, if my plans are cancelled or frustrated, if someone says something that hurts my feelings, I find it very easy to spend some unpleasant hours in discontent.

Jesus tells us not to be anxious about our plans because "your Father knows that you need them." The truth is, He knows better than we do just what we need.

Joseph Parker, one of England's great preachers in the last century, offers three reasons why things don't always go the way we'd like. First, he says, trials are useful. Trials often develop the best faculties of our nature, qualities that stir up our healthiest energy. We learn things through trials that we can't learn any other way.

The second thing, says Parker, is that even prosperity has its pains and its trials. There is no paradise on earth. Haven't you found it so—that the thing or place which seemed so attractive from a distance, when experienced or seen close up, had a flaw or two in it? "A thorn under every rose, a worm under every root," says Parker.

The third thing he adds is this: God knows exactly how much we can be trusted with. In other words, God knows what we need. "A contented spirit is a continual feast." That might be a good motto to put up on our walls. What can shake us if in our hearts we are content with God, with His work going on in us, with His plan for us today? It may be an easy lesson or a hard one that He sets before us, but He knows what we need and He always acts in love.

When God Seems Far Away   APRIL 24

Job 23 and Hebrews 4:12-16

*But He knoweth the way that I take: when He hath tried me,
I shall come forth as gold.*   JOB 23:10 (KJV)

WHAT A COMFORT THOSE WORDS HAVE BEEN to countless generations of God's people! And how many of us have inwardly cried out, "O that I knew where I might find Him!" There are none, I believe, who walk the way of faith who have not experienced times when God seems far distant and unreal. The saints and heroes of faith testify that they had to walk without the sweet assurance of His presence. David speaks of walking through the valley of the shadow of death. It is the picture of a time when things are dark, difficult, and very, very, threatening.

So we face a paradox here: we must learn to be honest and not deny those difficult times when God seems far away. We cannot be spiritual "Pollyannas" if we are to allow life's experiences to mature and bless us as God intends. On the other hand, we must not fail to follow Job's example in today's text, and say with him, "But He knoweth the way that I take; when He hath tried me, I shall come forth as gold." The fact that we do not "feel" that God is near does not negate the fact that He is near. He does not waver in His divine mercy toward us. But our broken, fractured lives in this world do not always clearly see or experience His love and closeness. It is a walk by faith, not by sight.

Do we really believe that all our days and all our ways are known to Him? Then we can say with Job, "He knoweth the way I take; when He hath tried me, I shall come forth as gold." God takes the long view. He has a goal in view, and your circumstances and mine are part of it. Even when He seems far away, we can choose to trust Him.

Help for the Long Haul   APRIL 25

Isaiah 63:7-9 and Hebrews 2:11-18

For because He Himself has suffered and been tempted, He is able to help those who are tempted.   HEBREWS 2:18 (RSV)

I will recount the steadfast love of the Lord.   ISA. 63:7A (RSV)

A S WE GET OLDER WE HAVE GREATER APPRECIATION for things that have endured. My wife and I recently took a trip to England, and one of the things that impressed us most was seeing the ancient, ordinary houses that have managed to stand for centuries.

I have a friend who had great difficulty giving up an old hat, and I remember how reluctant I am to discard shoes after they have stopped looking good.

The young, would-be athlete may hope to become an expert with the first throw of the ball, but it doesn't work that way. Endurance is to keep on trying, even when you miss the goal. A person who learns to play a musical instrument or to sing well must spend many, many hours in disciplined training—enduring in order to reach his desired end.

I remember people I have known through the years who had learned the secret of the long haul. They had decided, with the grace and help of God, to face life with courage, faith, and good cheer. I remember some of them even now—for as a pastor I used to call on them "to cheer them up," only to come away with much greater blessing than I had given. They taught me something about enduring.

We do not have to have "heroic" faith, super-strong characters, or the courage of lions. Our text reminds us that our Savior "has suffered and been tempted." And He knows the temptation to give in to despair and self-pity, along with other temptations. One of the worst is the temptation to believe that life is not worthwhile. That is not endurance—that is giving up. Yet, weak and needy as we may be, there is a secret source of strength available at this moment for our need, whatever it may be.

Sometimes the days will be filled with pleasant surprises. At other times, we will be tested by unpleasant circumstances. Yet He never leaves us, and "He is able to help." One of the best ways to arm ourselves for whatever may come is to "recount the steadfast love of the Lord."

Two Prayers—Two Answers   APRIL 26

Job 42:1-6 and 10-17 and Mark 10:46-52

Be of good comfort, rise; He calleth thee.   MARK 10:49B (KJV)

TODAY'S SCRIPTURES RECORD TWO ENCOUNTERS: Job's encounter with God, and the blind Bartimaeus with Jesus. In both cases sight is restored.

Let's go back a little to see the situations these two men faced. Job, as we know, has spent a good part of the first forty-one chapters of the book saying that if only God would appear, he would be justified before his accusing friends. Bartimaeus simply sat by the roadside begging.

We are not told who it was who went to Bartimaeus, but it was very likely one of Jesus' disciples. The important thing was their message: "Be of good comfort, rise. He calleth thee."

May I suggest to you who read this, whatever the circumstances you face, that this message is for you. Be of good comfort, rise. He calleth thee. First of all you are called to hope and faith. You do have a choice as to how you will handle your situation. Your problem can breed bitterness, fear, accusation against God or others, or it can become fertile ground in which the seed of faith produces the flower of hope. A good friend of mine is facing a prolonged bout of illness which keeps him from doing many things he wants to do. Prayers do not bring instant or quick healing. Yet, he says, he is finding treasures in his difficulty that he missed when life was all sunshine.

When we are told to be of good comfort and rise, we are being told that we can be of good cheer and rise above self-pity, depression, and gloom. Blessing awaits us when we answer His call and go to Him. Job repented of his former attitude, and said he had, in effect, been wrong in judging God! Bartimaeus walked away with new eyesight. Both men received what they needed.

Jesus never fails to give what we need. Be of good comfort, rise. He calleth thee.

You Shall Remember APRIL 27

Deuteronomy 8:11-20 and Matthew 5:43-48

You shall remember the Lord your God, for it is He who gives you power to get wealth; that He may confirm His covenant . . .
DEUTERONOMY 8:18 (RSV)

TODAY'S OLD TESTAMENT TEXT is part of Moses' last sermon to his people, in which he warns that in the good times to come they would be tempted to become proud and forgetful of God. They were like all other peoples of all times. When things are going our way, it is easy to begin to think that we're doing it ourselves and that we are doing pretty well. Then hard times come. They come to all of us, according to what God sees we need. In hard times He is teaching us how needy we really are, how dependent on Him we are. When we are healthy, we think little or nothing about it. But when our bodies refuse to cooperate and behave the way they should, then we are dependent on God. So, we learn an important truth in our need.

I have always had strong hands. The chores I did as a growing boy developed a good grip, and I found my hands would usually do almost anything I needed of them. Recently, however, quite suddenly, my left wrist became very painful. If it had been my right hand, I would have been seriously incapacitated. Fortunately, the condition did not last long. But I was suddenly faced with the fact that I could not expect always to have my strong hands doing just what I wanted them to do! It was not a pleasant confirmation.

What do we do with such experiences? We could become bitter, disconsolate, fearful. We could become passive and expect that "things can only get worse." Or we could "remember the Lord," that our strength really comes from Him. This verse has always meant a lot to me: *"As your days, so shall your strength be."*

That means that we will be given enough strength for the

demands of the day. We will have "strong hands" when we need them, and when we do not, there will be some other means to get through the day. For God does not lie, and He does not fail those who trust in Him; so we must not fail to give Him thanks.

A God Who Cares   APRIL 28

Revelation 7:9-17 and John 10:22-30

. . . and God will wipe away every tear from their eyes.
REVELATION 7:17B (RSV)

ISN'T THAT ONE OF THE MOST STRIKING, unforgettable scenes you could ever imagine? In the first part of today's passage from the Book of Revelation there is the description of the thousands and thousands of people from every tribe, tongue, kindred, and nation, shouting and singing their praises to God and to the Lamb. "Amen. Blessing and glory and wisdom and thanksgiving and honor and power and might be unto our God for ever and ever! Amen."

But it is when we come to the end of this chapter that we meet the most striking part of the scene. Can you remember when you were young, and fell and hurt yourself, or got into a fight with someone, or felt so bad over something that you began to cry—having your mother take a handkerchief, or her apron, and wipe away the tears from your eyes? Somehow you just felt better after that, even though nothing else had changed. Knowing she cared made the problem seem much more tolerable. Here is the great and majestic Almighty Father of all creation, lauded and praised by the unnumbered throngs, taking each one of us like a little child—each one who comes in hurt, disappointed with himself or herself, sad over something that he or she couldn't change—and He wipes *every* tear away. That is our God in all His tender love and mercy to us. That is the destiny that awaits His children. And our glimpse of it is meant to strengthen us, encourage our patience, and renew our desire to be more like Him. It is the picture of those who have forgotten to be sad.

So let us be cheerful, even now, knowing that the God who cares so much is our daily Companion, closer than breathing, nearer than hands or feet. His strength and comfort are ours if we will have them.

Everything She Had   APRIL 29

I Kings 17:8-16 and Mark 12:38-44

. . .[Jesus said,] "Truly I say to you, this poor widow has put in more than all those who are contributing to the treasury. For they contributed out of their abundance; but she out of her poverty has put in everything she had, her whole living."

MARK 12:43-44 (RSV)

WOULDN'T YOU LIKE TO KNOW what went on in the mind of this poor widow? People probably didn't even notice that she was there, much less care what she put into the treasury. And if you looked at it logically, wouldn't it seem strange for a poor person like her to throw her "living" into a treasury of such a magnificent place as the temple?

Some inner conversation must have been going on between her and God. Jesus watched, and knew. She was not giving her money to an organization. She was giving it to the Lord, trusting Him to use it for His purposes.

It is easy indeed to become calculating in our giving. The charlatans are always ready to prey on the unwary. So it pays to be careful in deciding where and what we give. But it doesn't pay to be "calculating" and "too careful" because, in so doing, we dry up the inner well which prompts the giving in the first place. Jesus has a word for us all here: He says that God makes

His sun to shine on the just and the unjust and his rain to fall on both. God, we might say, is a "careless" giver.

Paul's only direct quotation of Jesus in all his writings is: "It is more blessed to give than to receive." And Paul adds, "It is the cheerful giver that God loves."

So why did this poor widow throw in all she had? She believed in God. She believed that she was giving back to Him a token, an expression of her gratitude for His goodness. And so she gave.

We too, can give. Sometimes it will be material things. Sometimes it will be giving our time and attention to someone who needs it. There are many ways to give. God shows each of us the kind of giving best suited to our circumstances.

Don't let the springs of gratitude be dried up as you try to figure it all out. The widow had it right. She just followed the prompting of her heart. And Jesus saw it and was pleased.

Choosing to Rejoice   APRIL 30

Isaiah 61:10-62:3 and Luke 2:22-40

Text: I will greatly rejoice in the Lord, my soul shall exult in my God, for He has clothed me with the garments of salvation.
ISAIAH 61:10A (RSV)

REJOICING IS A MATTER OF CHOICE. Many who read these words may find it hard to believe that. Your circumstances may be such that *it feels* as though rejoicing is impossible. That's just what the devil would like you to believe! Nothing pleases him more than defeated, sad-faced Christians! The world will never believe in Jesus Christ if His disciples go around *choosing* to be glum instead of to rejoice.

Now, I'm not talking about some fake pretense at saying and acting as though "everything's OK." We might do that for a while, but sooner or later, reality will take over, and we'll have to face the dark side of things. Mary and Joseph certainly did as they fled Bethlehem, knowing that Herod was going to try to kill their infant Son. They had to make plans in a realistic way to get the Child out of harm's way. No, they were not afraid to look at the dark side of things, but that did not keep them from rejoicing in what God was doing! "Mary kept all these things and pondered them in her heart."

The prophet says, "I will greatly rejoice in the Lord." Whatever rejoicing we do "in the Lord" will stand us in good stead. It will drive away much of the false negativity we so easily accumulate. It will banish much of the fear of what might lie ahead. It will quicken our awareness of the love we have been shown *and are being shown* day by day. Believing that God really loves us, that He truly cares for us, is a great cause for rejoicing. What does it matter that we may have a few aches and pains? What does it matter if our bodies don't look or behave like they did twenty, thirty or fifty years ago? "I will greatly rejoice in the Lord."

Recount your blessings, and give thanks for them again. God has promised to go with you *through* all that lies ahead. So make that vital choice to "rejoice in the Lord."

Simple Trust

But I trust in your unfailing love; my heart rejoices in your salvation.

PSALM 13:5 (NIV)

On Death and Aging

As you grow older it is very important that you face the reality that your life has limits. Many of us do this naturally, but many of us also try to avoid this reality. You may only live another twenty years, another ten years, another five years. However many, the truth is, it's a short time. At my age, the next twenty years will go by fast. Many of my classmates and many members of my family have already died and with each of those deaths I have had to consider my own. As we age, the issue of our own death is something that we all must deal with.

How we face the question is not as important as is the willingness to raise the question in the first place. I mean, is death an issue at all? I think for most people it is not. Most people are not thinking at all about the fruitfulness of their life after death. More likely they are saying to themselves, "How can I live longer? My life is becoming less and less productive; I can do less and less and I might gradually become a burden to those around me." For some people the thought of having to be cared for is almost more than they can bear.

These are the sorts of issues that are very much on many people's minds as they age. Very few people, if any, are thinking that their death can be a *good* thing in the sense that Jesus meant it. But Jesus saw death, His own death in particular, as more than a way of getting from one place to another. He saw it as potentially fruitful in itself, and of benefit to His disciples. Very few people think about death the way Jesus thought about it.

So that is the first question: how can I prepare myself for my death in a way that I can make it a gift to others? To prepare for a good death I have to believe in a very deep way that I have something to offer to people beyond my life. I am a human being who was loved by God before I was born and who will be loved by God after I die. This life that I have is a very short period during which I can deepen my love for God and for people, but when I die, that love continues to be active. I am still in God's embrace. I prepare for my death then, first of all by claiming for myself the truth of who I am. I am someone who was alive in God's heart before I was born, and will be alive in God's heart after I die. When I die I know that I will depart from this brief life and that I will enter into a communion with God that, in some way, will allow me to keep nurturing the community on this earth.

Secondly, we must start shifting our thinking from successfulness to fruitfulness. We are living in a culture that measures the value of the human person by degrees of success: how much money do I make? how many friends do I have? what do my children do? have I won any trophies in this life? But when you grow older the value of all these successes gradually diminishes. You can't do certain things any more and you begin to feel more dependent, weaker, and more vulnerable. The challenge is to look at that vulnerability, not as a negative thing but as a positive thing—to look at it as a place where you can become fruitful.

It's very interesting: fruits are always the result of vulnerability. A child is conceived when two people are vulnerable with each other in their intimacy. Or the experience of peace and reconciliation can come when people are very honest and compassionate with one another, when they are vulnerable and open about their own needs and weaknesses. It is like breaking open the ground. We plow up the ground so that the seed that is sown there can grow. So, as we grow older, we have to move from thinking about ourselves in terms of successfulness to terms of fruitfulness.

Consider Jesus. When He died on the Cross, He had nothing left. Everything was taken from Him including His dignity. In the eyes of the world He was seen as a failure. His death on the Cross was the most vulnerable act conceivable, and it became the most fruitful in all history.

Henri Nouwen

Yet I Will Rejoice MAY 1

Habakkuk 3:2-6, 17-19 and Matthew 5:13-20

Though the fig tree does not blossom, nor fruit be on the vines,
the produce of the olive fail and the fields yield no food, the
flock be cut off from the fold and there be no herd in the stalls,
yet I will rejoice in the Lord, I will joy in the God
of my salvation. HABAKKUK 3:17, 18 (RSV)

THERE ARE CIRCUMSTANCES IN EACH OF OUR LIVES that could be occasion for discouragement, perhaps even despair. That is why this word of the prophet is so vital to us all. Life brings many difficult moments. The prophet here describes one in terms of a massive crop failure.

I remember back to a time when our family lived on a farm in North Carolina, and we experienced a drought so severe that the well dried up and we had no water for the livestock or ourselves. My father tried to find a place where he could dig a spring, but to no avail, and for some days, we carried water from a neighbor's well. I do not know if he despaired, because I was quite young. I know that it must have been an occasion for much prayer as well as effort on his part.

Looking back over the decades, I can see many situations where my own faith was tried, and where I had to fight my fear, because things were "out of control." Yet God never failed! The prophet knew this in order to put those words at the end of his little book. Though all these things happen, *yet I will rejoice in the Lord.*

In order to rejoice in the Lord, we have to have a basic faith in Him. We must know that He loves us and that sometimes His ways are beyond our understanding—but always, always, His ways are love. God is faithful, and His purpose is larger than the bumper crop we might want from this year's planting. He is growing a soul that will live with Him through all eternity.

"I will rejoice in the Lord" means that I will give thanks in remembering past mercies, present provisions, and future hope. He knows what He is doing, and He has set His love upon us. Armed with all that, we can fight the "blues," the self-pity, the resentment that things didn't work out the way we wanted them to. Though all things fail, *yet I will rejoice in the Lord!*

Rejoicing in Our Hope and Our Sufferings   MAY 2

Psalm 8 and Romans 5:1-5

We rejoice in our hope of sharing the glory of God. More than that, we rejoice in our sufferings. . . .   ROMANS 5:2B, 3A (RSV)

IT IS NOT SURPRISING THAT PAUL WOULD SAY that we rejoice in our hope. It *is* surprising that he would couple it with the statement that we rejoice *even more* in our sufferings.

I must begin by confessing that I have not yet fully learned to rejoice in my sufferings. Instead of tuning in immediately to a close communion with the Lord and asking Him to teach me what He has for me in this occasion, I run to fear and anxiety. I am, however, praying that through His infinite patience He will not give up on me, and will allow me to learn this all-important lesson: that nothing reaches us without His love, His promises, and His presence.

I have learned, however, over the years as a pastor, that many people I visited in their sickness or in their advanced years were far ahead of me in meeting suffering with courage and faith. They enlarged my horizons and gave me hope that there would be grace sufficient for my need when I could no longer have the control of my life which seems so natural when we are well and strong.

I attended a memorial service recently for a Christian minister, and at that service another minister spoke briefly about his friend. He said this beautiful, memorable word: "He did not escape, and neither shall we. We're *all* going to die," and paused to let it sink in. Then he added, "And we're all going to *live!*" That's the hope Paul is talking about: life that goes beyond our dying. Life that restores us to the relationship with God that he intended in the beginning: "Our hope of sharing the glory of God." When we immerse ourselves in that reality, and make our sufferings here take their proper place, we will be ready for the fulfillment of that Hope when God's time comes!

Keeping the Inner Self   MAY 3

Psalm 130 and Ephesians 4:25-5:2

Get rid of all bitterness, rage and anger . . . along with every
form of malice . . . and live a life of love.
EPHESIANS 4:31, 5:1A (NIV)

PSYCHOLOGISTS REMIND US THAT WE ARE GREATLY AFFECTED by our thoughts. The body does not live independently of the mind, and many experiments confirm that healthy thinking brings better health to the physical body. A person who for years nurses resentments and hurts ends up hurting himself or herself.

Paul is concerned that Christians guard their inner life. We talk about the world being a "dog eat dog" place, and surely there is much evidence that the competition in the world can be cruel indeed. But we Christians have learned a better way. We are told, "Be imitators of God as dearly loved children."

Our outward behavior is formed in our inner life. If we harbor dark and negative thoughts and feelings within, we will inevitably "leak" with grumpy and negative expressions. If we cultivate positive and faith-filled thoughts within, it will show by the way we take each day and the way we treat those around us.

One of the ways we can guard our inner life is by practicing praise. We can consciously and deliberately thank God for specific things every day. "This is the day the Lord *has* made. I will rejoice and *be grateful* in it." He has added another day to your life, and it will be filled with blessings. Many of them will be so small you might overlook them. But if you tune your mind and heart *to be grateful*, you will be surprised at how many good things come to you.

Then you can make a practice of *blessing* every person who enters your life that day. Henri Nouwen in his little book, *Life of the Beloved*, talks about the importance of blessing people. Something really happens when we convey to a person that he or she is a beloved person, a person for whom we care. We can strew blessings along the way we travel, like Johnny Appleseed. Long after we're gone, the fruit will be born. Don't forget to leave your blessings along the way!

Worthy MAY 4

Acts 9:1-20, Rev. 5:11-14, and John 21:1-19

Then I looked and I heard around the throne and the living crea-tures and the elders the voice of angels, numbering myriads of myriads and thousands of thousands, saying with a loud voice, "Worthy is the Lamb who was slain . . !" REV. 5:11, 12A (RSV)

WHAT A PICTURE WHICH JOHN SAW—that of the very high-est heaven engaged in worship and adoration of Jesus. In the imagery of the Old Testament, He is compared to the sacri-ficial lamb, the lamb which was offered to God as a means of finding forgiveness and cleansing from sin. Jesus became the "one, full, perfect sacrifice," for all people of all time, every-where, forever. He was God's provision to make us reconciled with Him and with ourselves.

He is always attentive to our hearts' cry, and He is merciful and kind to those who know they have sinned. There is a con-tinuing stream of praise in Scripture which reaches its climax in this final book, the Revelation to St. John.

Sometimes we wonder why we should spend time praising

and worshipping. Let me offer several reasons: First, because He is worthy. We can never repay Him for His grace and mercy, but we can love Him and adore Him for it. Second, because praise is good for us. God has so made us that we actually thrive inwardly as we learn to give thanks and worship freely. Something bottled up in us gets released, and we become freer, healthier, happier people. Third, our praise gladdens others. The vision of heaven is a vision of uncountable throngs "lost in wonder, love, and praise." There is something really thrilling and joyful about a large number of people joined in praise. (We even see this on a human level as crowds cheer on and applaud their favorite team or athlete.) Last fall, I attended a large rally where there were 13,000 Christians singing songs of praise. It was a joy and blessing to hear others praising God.

Finally, our praise helps us through the hard places. When we're struggling with those old plaguing problems that annoy us, praise can help us get through. We have the key to unlock the prison of despair and hopelessness *if* we will use it. That key is praise! We, too, can join that everlasting song, singing in our hearts, "Worthy! Worthy is the Lamb who was slain!"

Songs in the Night   MAY 5

Acts 16:16-34 and John 17:20-26

But about midnight Paul and Silas were praying and singing hymns to God, and the prisoners were listening to them.
ACTS 16:25 (RSV)

THIS WONDERFUL STORY OF PAUL AND SILAS in the Philippian jail is a great illustration of how Paul and the other Christians of that day were able to stand against such suffering and persecution without giving up their faith. They praised their way through!

There are many places in the New Testament where we are

taught the importance of praise and thanksgiving, and I can see here that it is one of the ways we prepare ourselves to face hard times.

I am old enough to remember when our country went through what was often referred to as "hard times." In those days before World War II, many people were struggling to keep afloat financially; yet in spite of all the hardships people faced, they were often cheerful and hopeful. It depended on the inner attitude more than the given circumstance.

Whenever there seem to be reasons to complain or feel sorry for ourselves, there are many more reasons for songs in the night. God's love is constant and true, and we are never left to face anything alone. Looking back over the years, can we not see His gracious hand in how we were led, protected, and provided for—even when we had no conscious knowledge of it? His bounty provided. And so, as we give thanks, as we sing in our hearts our songs of praise, we are strengthened, as Paul and Silas were.

One of the other great things about this story that always strikes me is this: it seems almost in answer to their songs that the earthquake came, shook the foundations, and then "everyone's chains fell off." It is not too much of an exaggeration to see more than physical chains falling away. The chains of fear, resentment, bitterness or despair that can bind us are not strong enough to remain in the face of our heartfelt praise. Those songs in the night are more than something with which to pass the time. They are weapons in our spiritual warfare. They are really songs of victory!

Good News of a Great Joy   MAY 6

Micah 5:2-4 and Luke 1:39-49

*And the angel said to them, "Be not afraid; for behold I bring
you good news of a great joy which will come to all the people."*
LUKE 2:10 (RSV)

THIS IS THE CHRISTMAS MESSAGE. It is always "good news"
and it always brings "great joy" to those who believe it and
receive it.

The message comes to us in the midst of our fears. Of
course the shepherds were afraid, because they were not used to
seeing angels, and who would not tremble before such a sight?
There were other fears too—fears with which they lived all the
time. We know them. There are fears of unnamed, almost sub-
conscious troubles that might await us tomorrow. Most people
know of those. And they are even more present when we are
going through some difficult period or some question of bodily
health. So Christmas has good news for those who are afraid.

What is that news? It is that God loves us so much that He
has come down to dwell with us. Jesus' birth is a sign, a sign
that God has not abandoned this poor world and its people. It
is a sign that He cares for us. No other reason would cause Him
to send His beloved Son to become one of us.

Christmas inaugurates a new situation. Since God has
come to dwell with men, and since Jesus Christ came to this
earth, things have never been the same. We are thousands of
miles from Bethlehem, and two thousand years beyond the
time this story takes place. Yet the world "pauses" to celebrate
this birth with bright colors, hanging greens, and lights—often
not realizing all that we are doing. We are celebrating a *fact*
that "God so loved the world that He gave His only begotten
Son."

I know that many of you face hard situations, uncertain
days, sometimes weary, lonely times. But this message comes
with a prayer that your heart will be open to hear the word the

angel spoke to the shepherds: "Do not be afraid. For behold, I bring you good news of a great joy." May the one who lay in the Bethlehem stable find a place of rest and welcome in your heart.

Making Prayer with Joy MAY 7

Philippians 1:1-11 and LUKE 3:1-6

I thank my God in all my remembrance of you, always in every prayer of mine for you all making my prayer with joy.
PHILIPPIANS 1:3 (RSV)

PAUL GIVES US A GLIMPSE OF HIS RELATIONSHIP with this church to which he was writing. Apparently they had remained loyally committed to helping him in his ministry through some very hard times. We can appreciate how he must have felt when he prayed for them.

Do you make your prayer with joy? Do you allow memory to do its part, and bring to your mind the blessings God has given you through the people who have been part of your life? If you do, you will be immeasurably enriched. Recalling their kindness helps to bring joy today. It may be a kindness of yesterday, or of forty years ago. Its memory will shed a softening, warming, glowing joy to your heart. And in such a state, your prayers will be more fervent and effectual.

Paul shows that kind of joy. He is in prison, but that does not matter. Many of you are confined by bodily ailments or weakness, so that you cannot move about as you would like. But Paul's spirit was not confined or restrained. He could reach out in his heart and mind to those who had blessed him, he could love them, show concern for them, and pray for them "with joy."

I know no better remedy for self-pity and the negative spirit with which we all have to fight at times than an active choice to give thanks, to praise, to lift up the heart in joyful memory of blessings received. That prepares us to receive blessings yet to come.

Praise, thanksgiving, "Prayer with joy." What a difference they make!

Remembrance and Thanksgiving MAY 8

Psalm 111 and Luke 2:22-40

He has caused His wonderful works to be remembered; the Lord is gracious and merciful. PSALM 111:4 (RSV)

R EMEMBERING THE PAST CAN BE A BLESSING, providing we do not use it to escape from the present. Remembering and telling others about the blessings God has given us can be a way of strengthening their faith as well as our own.

Many comedians make a sourcebook of comedy out of their remembrance of things from their childhood. They have the ability to turn what may have been painful experiences into hilarious accounts. Others identify with their confusion or their mistakes, and everybody gets a good laugh. These people have learned not to take themselves too seriously! When you think back on "life's most embarrassing moments"—didn't much of the pain come from taking yourself too seriously in the situation? Looking back, it is possible to laugh a healing, freeing kind of laugh—knowing that it didn't make *that* much difference after all.

On the other hand, I have known people who made themselves sick or kept themselves sick by rehearsing old hurts. Sometimes people have a whole list of things they are still angry about. One person was fuming about things that happened thirty years ago—and it was obvious in listening to her that she had never forgiven anyone in the situation nor taken any responsibility for it herself. That is the wrong kind of remembering! Unless we learn to forgive those who have hurt, betrayed or disappointed us, we will remain stuck in destructive feelings that can literally cripple us as we get older. Look well to clean out old resentments. Forgive! Forgive!

There is, however, a time for memories cherished. It does not need to be a vain clinging to the past, but a gentle and heartwarming time that gives us hope and strength for the present. God is at work in our lives every day, seeking to make us more what we were created to be. He has given us many things just because He loves us and cares for us. So, remember—a little flower someone gave you; a new pen, or shirt, or magazine; an unexpected visit from someone you love; a kind deed by a neighbor or friend; a book you enjoyed, a movie you liked; a song or a sermon that made you love God more. Thousands of blessings—to be remembered—with thanksgiving!

Mother and Child MAY 9

Isaiah 7:10-16 and Matthew 1:18-25

Behold, a virgin shall conceive and bear a son
and shall call His name Immanuel. ISA. 7:14B (KJV)

"And you shall call His name Jesus, for He will save
His people from their sins." MATT. 1:21B (RSV)

THE CHRISTMAS SCRIPTURES SAY SOMETHING important about motherhood. Most of you who read these lines were brought up in a time when mothers were honored and respected in a special way. Motherhood was held to be one of the greatest privileges of womanhood, and to be a good mother meant to do something significant for the welfare of the world and the future of humanity. Perhaps at times the concept was romanticized, and a bit overdone at times, but there was something quite sound in honoring the role mothers have played in all our lives and in the life of our human race.

Mary forever remains the model of motherhood—from the moment the angel announced what was to come, right through to the time she stood by the cross watching her Son die—she entered fully into God's call. Much of her work and her role in training Jesus is hidden from view, but is there nonetheless. We can offer thanks to God for her faithfulness, and remember our mothers and the often hidden ways they affected our lives.

Mother and child. Can there be any more tender, disarming picture? Is any relationship more beautiful? The Son of God Himself, co-Creator of the universe, Lord of heaven and earth, is being cradled in His mother's arms. He receives her loving care and is nurtured by it. This is a great sign and wonder.

God is all-sufficient, and could create a thousand worlds if He chose. Yet in His grace and mercy toward us, He chose to come to us in this helplessness as an Infant. Not only so, He chose to allow us to love Him tenderly and to receive His tender love—just as He loved His mother and was loved by her. He calls us His brothers and sisters, and says that "whoever does the will of God is my mother and my sister and my brother," and graciously admits us into this tender, loving relationship that He knew with His own mother. Since each of us yearns for this kind of love deep within, He desires to lead us to a closer, more loving relationship with Himself—"Love's pure light."

Strange Blessings! MAY 10

Psalm 1 and Luke 16:17-26

Blessed are you poor . . . you that hunger, . . .you that weep now. . . . Blessed are you when men hate you. . . . LUKE 6:20-22 (RSV)

THESE SAYINGS OF JESUS HAVE ALWAYS GIVEN Christians trouble—if we have really studied them. They turn upside down the things we associate with happiness.

Jesus is not telling us to *love* to be poor, hungry or sad, or to have people hate us. That would be a kind of soul sickness—even dangerous. Rather, He is facing a situation in which people *are* in need, poor, sad, and at times, hated by others. He is saying that such people are blessed because God has something in store for them which they are to seek first.

This Scripture goes on to add four "woes" to these four "blesseds" and cautions us against getting our eyes fixed on material prosperity, bodily comfort and the esteem of the world. Such goals will always betray us in the end. Life is meant to be more than food, comfort and the esteem of others!

I do not like bodily pain! I suppose that's a fairly common reaction. And I would like the security of enough money to meet expenses and needs—I don't think that is evil. But when I have had to face bodily discomfort, serious illness, or an uncertain future—I have found God is there, and that He more than compensates for what He asks me to bear.

Jesus was not playing games when He said those who suffer should consider themselves "blessed." There is much to be learned in the shadow of illness, in the uncertainty of what life holds, in the limitations our circumstances may impose on us. Learning about the faithfulness of a faithful God and experiencing the "peace that passes understanding"—surely these are blessings that cannot be numbered.

So wherever you are today, and whatever you may be asked to accept from your Heavenly Father, know of surety that He intends it to bless you with it.

My Hope is Built   MAY 11

I Thessalonians 1:1-10 and Matthew 22:34-46

. . . You turned to God from idols, to serve a living and true
God, and to wait for His Son from heaven, whom He raised
from the dead, Jesus who delivers us from the wrath to come.
I THESS. 1:9B-10. (RSV)

IN THIS LETTER TO THE CHRISTIANS in Thessalonica, Paul
makes note that this little group of people had heard the Good
News, had *believed* it, and had found that it made a great difference in their lives.

Every one of us has been on a journey or we might say, a
pilgrimage, in our lives. The journey may have been smooth, or
it may have been fraught with many unexpected and unwelcome turns and rough places. But whatever it was for you, it is
your own story and it is important to see God's part in it.

From time to time in recent months I have looked back over
the decades of my life. Memories bring both sadness and joy,
both repentance and gratitude. When I think of times where I
might have made a bad choice or did something that brought
great difficulty or pain to another person, I ask forgiveness of
the Lord and *accept* His forgiveness. When I see God's hand in
some event or turn in my life, I can truly praise and thank Him,
even when, at the time, I had no consciousness that He was leading or guiding. It is like Jacob, when he was running away from
Esau, and spent the night at Bethel where he saw a dream/vision.
He said, "Surely God is in this place and I knew it not." That's
the way it is when we look back at many places in our lives. We
can say, "Surely God was there, and I didn't know it." The fact
that we can realize it now is a good thing, for we can give Him
thanks and praise, even if it is long overdue.

We can all give thanks that, somewhere along our journey,
we, like the Thessalonians, "turned to God from idols." We
were blessed with the Good News of God's love, and by His

grace, we believe in it, accept it, and "wait for His Son from heaven . . . Jesus . . ." That is enough to live on!

When Hearts are Troubled   MAY 12

Revelation 21:10, 21:22-22:5 and John 14:23-29

Peace I leave with you; my peace I give to you; not as the world gives do I give to you. Let not your hearts be troubled, neither let them be afraid.   JOHN 14:27 (RSV)

MANY OF US HAVE CIRCUMSTANCES IN OUR LIVES that are worrisome. We do not know what the future will hold in the next few months or years. In situations like that it is easy to give in to worry and fear.

Fear is a natural response to the unknown. It is even a healthy response in some situations, warning of dangers that may be there. But fear of the unknown can get out of hand. Instead of building on God's protection over us and His goodness to us through all our days, we may let ourselves be overrun with fearfulness.

Jesus was concerned about the fears His friends were facing as He talked with them about His imminent departure. Their faith was going to be put to the test. Would it stand up? Not without some help from Him. So He promised "my peace I give to you." In the same way, I believe He is concerned about us and our fears, and makes the same promise. We may have to confess our lack of trust and make the choice not to entertain the harassing thoughts about what the future *might* hold. Then we can center our minds on what we know Him to be. "Thou wilt keep him in perfect peace whose mind is stayed on Thee."

When I was a small boy, I remember waking up and being afraid of the dark—until I remembered that my father was nearby. Fear would vanish and the dark would lose its terror. Life teaches us many lessons through the years. One of the most important is this: the Lord is on our side. He will not fail us in our hour of need. Stay with the present moment, and don't let foolish thoughts destroy the reality of the peace He is offering you now.

God is God   MAY 13

Exodus 3: 12-16 and I Corinthians 3:10-15

For no one can lay any foundation other than the one already laid, which is Jesus Christ. I CORINTHIANS 3:11 (NIV)

TODAY'S GOSPEL READING WARNS US that it is not enough to say, "Lord, Lord." Someone recently said to some of us, "You have created a Jesus of your own making, not the real Jesus. And when He does something that doesn't correspond to the image you have made of Him, you go into doubt and confusion." I think that applies to many of us. Jesus warns us in this parable that God is God, and that we must take seriously what He has told us if we want to be members of His kingdom.

This is not a negative thing, though. The image which we have sometimes worked out for ourselves is a weak, ineffectual "god" of our own making, and not able to deliver us when we are in real need. Our home-made gods turn out to be mean and petty, selfish and cruel in the long run. Some people even created a "god" who is ready to punish them at "the drop of a hat" so to speak, and are greatly afraid of it. But God, the true God whom Jesus reveals to us is more merciful and gracious than any of us could imagine Him to be. The hymn writer says it like this:

> For the love of God is broader
> Than the measure of man's mind,
> And the heart of the eternal
> Is most wonderfully kind.

We are building the house of our souls day by day. Is that house on the firm foundation of simple childlike trust in Jesus Christ and a desire to belong to Him? If it is to stand in the storms, it cannot rest on our own goodness, our moral standards, our honesty, truthfulness, or decency. Paul says "No other foundation can anyone lay than that which is laid, which is Jesus Christ." (ICor. 3:11)

He Remains Faithful   MAY 14

II Timothy 2:8-15 and Luke 17:11-19

If we are faithless, He remains faithful—for He cannot deny Himself. II TIM. 2:13 (RSV)

IT IS ALWAYS A JOY AND PRIVILEGE TO WRITE OR SPEAK about the faithfulness of God! The older I get, the greater and more wonderful the privilege seems. That may be in part because as we get older, we accumulate more "evidence" as it were, of that faithfulness.

It is good, as the Bible tells us, to rehearse the blessings God has bestowed on us. You remember how Israel, after that amazing miracle of deliverance through the Red Sea, accused Moses of leading them out to perish after just three days in the wilderness! It would be easy to judge them if we were not so much like them. We easily forget the many ways in which God's blessing are poured out on us.

I find the remembrance of God's faithfulness in my life is often coupled with the sad truth that I was not always faithful to Him. My own ambitions, personal wishes, "the devices and desires of my own heart" often spoke louder than any latent desire to be "ever faithful, ever true." Looking back, I can see that even in my best moments there were elements of pride, ambition and personal gain that sullied what I thought were spiritually faithful decisions. That would be a "downer" if it were not for the faithful mercy of God! If we had to look only at where we have not measured up, and did not know that God's mercies are over all His works, we might get very distressed, discouraged and depressed.

But His interest is not in keeping strict accounts. He wants a people who are learning from their mistakes, pressing on and trusting that He will never let them down. I heard a black gospel choir at a meeting in Washington, D.C. singing "He's never failed me yet!" That's my testimony, and I suspect it's yours as well!

And He Believed the Lord — MAY 15

Genesis 15:1-6 and Hebrews 11:1-2, 8-16

And he [Abraham] believed the Lord; and He reckoned it to him as righteousness. GENESIS 15:6 (KJV)

LET'S BE HONEST ABOUT IT. It's not always easy to believe God. Sometimes it is hard even to believe *in* God. So much in the world seems to go on without Him. He seems removed from much of the tragedy, the sin, the horrors of life. Faith does not always come easy.

Yet there is a vital connection between what we believe and what we are. We can't separate the two. People tend to become like what they believe.

Abraham's faith in God brought him through some very hard times. There were times when he made mistakes, but God never failed him. An ultimate test was his willingness to sacrifice his beloved son, Isaac, because he trusted God. So God "counted it to him as righteousness." Our simple faith is pleasing to God.

We can make the same kind of choice—to trust when things are hard. God has never failed us. He has never asked us to do anything that was to our hurt. Some things we may have faced were very difficult and our faith may have been shaken. That's all right because easy "Pollyanna" faith has to be matured, and maturity comes through the hard times. We do not have to understand everything that happens, but we can find God is still our refuge and strength, a very present help in trouble.

Abraham chose to believe in God. Sometimes other choices may seem easier, less costly. But in the end, if we choose to believe God, that choice brings great reward and great joy. You, too, can make that choice today.

Choosing Masters   MAY 16

I Timothy 2:1-7 and Luke 16:1-13

No servant can serve two masters; for either he will hate the one and love the other, or he will be devoted to the one and despise the other. You cannot serve God and mammon.
LUKE 16:13 (RSV)

WHAT A SHOCK IT IS TO REALIZE THAT, no matter what we may think, we are going to serve one master or the other. Many people labor under the delusion that they can be free from all masters. But it just isn't so. If we choose, we can become servants of God.

Whichever master we choose is going to lay down the rules of servanthood. And Jesus says, "Learn of me; for my yoke is easy and my burden is light." His "easy yoke" means we must learn to love with His love, denying ourselves and allowing the cross to work in our lives.

The other master, the god of Mammon, is the world spirit—the spirit that claims to set us free but actually enslaves us to the cares and burdens of a world in rebellion. Our appetites cannot be satisfied with the things of this world, because we were made for God. The world teases us with its "charms," but always leaves us empty and unsatisfied. The distressing disorder of our cities, the frantic search for pleasure through drugs, alcohol, and sex by many, even the music of our age—all characterize this frantic despair. Mammon is a bad master.

What about those of us who haven't chosen that route? How do we still make wrong choices and choose the wrong master? Every time we give in to worry, fretting or complaining about our lot; every time we accuse God in our minds of not being fair, not being loving, not caring about where we are or what is happening—we are in truth choosing mammon instead of God.

Is your future solidly in the keeping of your heavenly Father? If not, you are choosing the wrong master. Make this prayer your own by praying it over and over again: "For all that is past I praise you; for all that is to come, I trust you." Choose the Master who loves you and who gave His life that you might enjoy eternal life in His service forever.

Where You Go I Will Go   MAY 17

Ruth 1:1-119A and I Thessalonians 1:1-10

. . . Entreat me not to leave you or to return from following you,
for where you go I will go, and where you lodge I will lodge;
your people shall be my people, and your God my God.
RUTH 1:16 (RSV)

THIS VERSE IS FROM THE BEAUTIFUL STORY of a foreign widow who followed the inner promptings of her heart to leave her native people and become an Israelite.

But for me these words also speak to quite different situations. They come from the heart. They are the words of the faithful soul spoken to our Savior Jesus Christ.

Many things would "entreat" us to leave Him. We have no external proof that He will always bless us and meet our needs. If we follow Him, it must be by faith, not by sight. The clouds of doubts, the darkness of the unknown, the questions that arise in the face of grief and loss, the anxiety of sickness—all these can whisper their invitation to "return from following" Him. Many of Jesus' disciples drew back because His saying put more on them than they wanted. So they "returned from following" Him.

The world keeps trying to tell us that selfishness is the way to get the most out of life. Recently an elderly man was being interviewed about his Social Security. He admitted that he didn't really *need* Social Security. He was quite well-off without it. But his attitude was sad: "I want every penny coming to me and I would never, never agree to have it lessened!" He obviously bought the idea that the meaning of life is to "take care of #1." And all of us are tempted to think that.

So why would we say with Ruth, "Where you go I will go, and where you lodge I will lodge"? The answer is simple. Ruth had found Naomi a trustworthy mother. She had seen Naomi's faith at work in everyday circumstances, and knew it would hold up. That was enough for her. Have you and I not had enough experience with Jesus Christ to know that He is utterly and completely trustworthy? When we look at His life, His death, and His present help, we want to say, "Yes, Lord, where You go I will go. Your God will be my God." And so may it be.

The Pursuit of Happiness   MAY 18

Galatians 5:6, 13-25 and Luke 9:51-62

But the fruit of the Spirit is love, joy, peace, patience, kindness, goodness, faithfulness, gentleness, self-control.
GAL. 5:22,23A (RSV)

A SIGN OUTSIDE A CHURCH I PASSED RECENTLY READ: "Happiness is an inside job."

That sign set me thinking about the simple but profound

truth it contained. I thought of the times I have been miserable in very comfortable surroundings. I thought of people I have known who had everything, from a worldly viewpoint—money, friends, material goods, social standing—and yet were desperately unhappy.

In his letter to the Galatians, Paul tells us that "love, joy, and peace" are the fruit of the Spirit of God living and dwelling in our hearts. Of course there is a difference between "happiness" and "joy." Our surface emotions are dependent on outward circumstances. We cannot be happy if something terrible is happening to people we love, or if our situation is suddenly one of danger, and so on. We feel fear, grief, sadness—possibly even worry or anxiety.

But Paul is talking about something deeper—something that can be compared to the ocean. On the surface the storm churns up waves—sometimes mighty ones. But go deep enough and there is stillness, calm, unruffled quiet. So it is meant to be with us.

We remember the story of Jesus with His disciples on the stormy sea of Galilee. In fear and panic when they thought the boat was going to capsize, they woke Jesus and gave Him a mild rebuke for "deserting them" in their hour of need. How like us! Then He spoke His word and the sea became calm.

"Happiness is an inside job." Are we dwelling in the reality of His joy, love, and peace, or are we allowing outward events to control our inner moods and emotions? We do have choices, even when we see we have fallen into old, nonproductive patterns. If we are tempted to be grumpy (or find that we are already grumpy), fearful, or resentful about something we cannot change, we can *inwardly* go to the Lord in prayer and ask for His peace, His joy, and His love to flow into us. Elizabeth Barrett Browning said, "Round our restlessness, His rest." Knowing that He is in charge can change our outlook, and that can make all the difference!

Promise, Hope, and Preparation   MAY 19

Zechariah 14:4-9 and Luke 21:25-31

. . . When you see these things taking place, you know
that the kingdom of God is near.   LUKE 21:31 (RSV)

THE BIBLE NEVER BLINKS AT THE HARD REALITIES OF LIFE. It does not attempt to cover them up with deceptive, cosmetic colors. The writers know and accept the bewilderment we sometimes feel when the conditions of life "cave in" on us—the presence of pain, discomfort, poverty, injustice, and sufferings of various kinds. These things are not hidden from their eyes. And this makes the Bible, of all books, the most practical down-to-earth guide for us.

Today's Gospel is taken from Jesus' words spoken during the last week of His earthly life. Jesus' earthly mission is almost finished. His race is almost run. And now His disciples, with only a foreboding about what might lie ahead, need some word from Him. What is that word? A strong word of hope. When these frightening things begin to happen, He says, you know that the kingdom of God is near. Worlds are colliding, kingdoms of this world with all their darkness, rebellion, and cruelty clash with the Kingdom of God, with its light and truth. Darkness may seem temporarily to be winning. But don't worry! God will be King over the whole earth. His Kingdom is drawing near!

We don't have to wait to see world kingdoms clashing and falling, systems of government coming apart. We find enough calamity in our individual lives with just the ordinary things that happen to us all to make this word a welcome one. Chaos and calamity do not have the last word. There is a God in Heaven and that God is still in charge. Is it safe to go on in faith and hope, because He has shown His love for us in Jesus Christ? Some day Christ will come again and take the power and glory which is His due. Until that day, we can trust Him, love Him, and obey Him and live in His kingdom.

Attitudes Matter!   MAY 20

Numbers 11:4-20 and Mark 9:38-50

And the people of Israel also wept again and said: "O that we had meat to eat! We remember . . ."   NUMBERS 11:4B, 5A (RSV)

Have salt in yourselves and be at peace with one another.
MARK 9:50B (RSV)

WHAT A TIME GOD HAD IN LEADING HIS PEOPLE into their rightful inheritance! Along the way their dissatisfaction and murmuring kept getting them into trouble.

We may smile when we read that in the desert they began to fantasize about the free fish, the cucumbers, onions, and garlic they had enjoyed in Egypt. Apparently they had forgotten the terrible suffering that went along with their slavery! And the truth is, human beings haven't changed much. We are all like those children of Israel. It's wonderful to be able to look back and recall the pleasant things of the past, but we cannot afford to let ourselves murmur and complain about the present, as though God had done some terrible thing to us by allowing our present situation.

Some years ago, circumstances in my life changed, and the thing that I had been doing for a quarter of a century I could no longer do. I longed to get back to the way things were, but I would forget that there were many stresses and hurts connected with my former position. I thought of the pleasant fulfillment. But my good wife would remind me of the reality that God had brought to an end. It was one of the hardest lessons of my life, and I almost missed it through stubborn insistence on "going back" to the way things had been.

I am sure that many who read these lines are tempted in like manner to view the past with rose-colored glasses and to view the present with some tinge of bitterness or dissatisfaction. If that is true, I urge you to hear the Lord's words: "Have salt in yourselves and be at peace with one another." This refers to an attitude that says, "Sometimes I get tired of the way things are. But I choose to accept that God knows best and He is in charge of my life." Attitudes do matter, and they can make all the difference—no matter what the outward circumstances may be. And, in truth, God *is* still in charge. We can be thankful for that!

To Bind Up the Brokenhearted MAY 21

Isaiah 61:1-4 and Acts 8:14-17

The Spirit of the Lord God is upon me . . .; He has sent me to bind up the brokenhearted . . . to comfort all who mourn.
ISAIAH 61:1, 2B (RSV)

IN THE FULLNESS OF TIME, GOD SENT HIS SON to fulfill the promises He had made to His people. And among the most treasured of those is the word from this text. He was sent to bind up the brokenhearted and to comfort those who mourn.

Everyone of us has experienced brokenheartedness. It may be from the loss of a husband or wife—a parent or a child. It may come from the loss of a friend, or from some misunderstanding or rejection. These losses make deep wounds and require deep healing. Whatever our loss, we all know the feeling of the "broken heart."

The wonderful promise is that Jesus has come to heal. He does this by giving us His Holy Spirit to comfort and strengthen us and to "bind up" the wound. We may even come to see that in the larger wisdom and providence of God the very thing which hurt so badly was actually for the best.

This is not a conclusion to be arrived at lightly or hastily, because we need to have healthy grief over the things that hurt us. Otherwise we may just repress our memories of them and leave them like a festering wound that stops hurting for the moment but stays on to cause trouble later. One of the worst things that can come of a broken heart is a bitter spirit. When it is not healed, we may nurse a deep-rooted bitterness that plagues us and darkens our whole outlook on life. When we are struggling with a broken heart we need to draw aside with Jesus and give it to Him. We do not know how He is able to heal, but we know that He can—and *does*.

There is yet another kind of brokenheartedness. Psalm 51 says, "A broken and contrite heart, O God, Thou wilt not despise." *That* kind of broken heart comes from a deep awareness of our own wrongness and our sin. And that kind of broken heart is healed by the miracle of forgiveness. "He has sent me to bind up the brokenhearted."

Rejoicing Anyhow   MAY 22

Proverbs 8:22-31, Romans 5:1-5, and John 16:12-15

More than that, we rejoice in our sufferings, . . . because God's love has been poured into our hearts through the Holy Spirit which has been given to us ROMANS 5:3A, 5B (RSV)

I'M NOT VERY GOOD AT SUFFERING. When something happens to me or to someone close to me, it upsets me greatly inside. Nor do I enjoy pain. And I don't like having to do what I'm told—whether it's having to go to the dentist or for a medical examination or taking a blood test—or having to eat someone else's choice when I had set my heart on something else. Such is the stuff of our old self-centered nature. What can be done about it?

Paul says in his letter the Philippians, "I have learned to be content with whatever state I am in—poverty or need, plenty or famine." That's quite something! In this passage today he says that we have been given grace through Jesus Christ to stand (not give up!) and we rejoice in the hope of sharing God's glory. And then he adds, "*More than that*, we rejoice in our sufferings." Does that mean he enjoyed suffering? I don't think so! I think he had learned a secret of meeting suffering with something more than anger, resentment or self-pity. He looked beyond and saw that God was using the suffering to work something great and good in us—and "hope does not disappoint us."

Suffering is an inevitable part of life. It does not have to defeat you. In fact, it can be the anvil upon which you become a more beautiful work of God. Let us all pray for one another that we may learn better to "rejoice in our sufferings," and in spite of them, "rejoice anyhow!"

Yearning for God's Peace   MAY 23

Psalm 29 and Mark 1:4-11

May the Lord give strength to His people! May the Lord bless His people with peace.   PSALM 29:11 (RSV)

PEACE IS MUCH ON OUR MINDS THESE DAYS, with the turmoil which continues to rage in the world. Peace is a common human longing—whether it be for peace among nations or peace in our families, or peace in our hearts. We have a "built-in" longing for it.

I am reminded of a beautiful hymn by Adelaid Procter in which she thanks God for the shadows as well as the sunshine. There is great wisdom in that: Too many blessings with too little suffering can lead to a calloused heart. The softening effect of our human frailty makes our hearts more receptive to God's tender wooing. He created us to find our peace in Him, and when we tire of seeking fulfillment in other ways, He waits for us to find where that "deeper peace" is to be found. When the psalmist prays, "May the Lord bless His people with peace," I believe he has in mind the "peace which passes understanding" which we have "in the midst of trouble." Our world is not a place of permanent peace. It is fraught with sin—expressed in a thousand different ways, and as long as this reigns in the hearts of men and women, there will be no lasting peace.

But we can know a peace which the world cannot give and cannot take away. It is the peace of heart we have through our faith in Jesus Christ. It is His gift to us as we truly turn to Him. May that peace stand guard over us all, in greater and greater measure.

When God Speaks to Us   MAY 24

Psalm 85 and Philippians 3:4B-14

Let me hear what God the Lord will speak, for He will speak peace to His people.   PSALM 85:8 (RSV)

WHEN GOD SPEAKS TO US, HIS WORD BRINGS PEACE. This is an encouraging word for all of us. "He will speak peace to His people." What is that peace, and what are its component parts? *First,* there is a sense of rest and ease with God. Sometimes His word is a sharp word, piercing our hearts with stabbing awareness of how wrong we have been—how neglectful, how stubborn, how opinionated, how unloving. It may be painful, but then comes the joyful awareness that we are forgiven, that we do not have to live with guilt. And with that awareness comes a new sense of "at-one-ness" with God and with ourselves.

Think of all the conditions that bring uneasiness to our souls. There are many circumstances which we would consider the opposite of peace: sin, thronging duties, sorrows, absence of loved ones, uncertain future. We live in a very uncertain age, and with news instantly available to us on TV, we are all too aware of the spasms and convulsions of a tortured and evil age. An old evening prayer reads: Be present, O merciful God, and protect us through the silent hours of this night; so that we who are wearied by the changes and chances of this world may rest on Thy eternal changelessness; through Jesus Christ our Lord."

Are we as aware as we should be of the "eternal changeless-ness" of God?

The peace which God speaks makes us content with cir-cumstances we cannot change. Suffering may consist in being where we would not choose to be, or having conditions in our lives which are very contrary to our desires. Someone said, "Peace does not dwell in outward things, but in the soul. We may perceive it in the midst of the bitterest pain, if our will remains firm and submissive." If things cannot be changed, we need to come to peace by submitting to a will higher than our own. "Let me hear what the Lord will speak for He will speak peace to His people."

I Have Seen the Lord   MAY 25

Colossians 3:1-14 and John 20:1-18

Mary Magdalene went and said to the disciples, "I have seen the Lord"; and she told them that He had said these things to her.
JOHN 20:18 (RSV)

MARY MAGDALENE WENT TO JESUS' TOMB expecting only to show her abiding love and gratitude for what He had done for her. She had been an emotionally unstable, tormented soul before Jesus healed her and brought her hope. She had been a harlot. But her sins were no barrier to the Savior. He saw her need and He reached out to her.

Now Jesus was gone. Nothing remained but the lifeless body, hastily placed in the tomb just before sunset on Friday. When the Sabbath was over, Mary rose early to go to the tomb. The other Gospels tell us that Mary went with other women, taking spices they had prepared, hoping someone would roll away the stone over the door so they might anoint His Body in their final act of love for Him.

Not mentioning the other women, John shows us Mary

Magdalene, "weeping outside the tomb." When figures inside the tomb asked her why she was weeping, she answered, "They have taken away my Lord, and I do not know where they have laid Him."

Then someone she took to be the gardener spoke, asking the same question. Her answer was, "Sir, if you have taken Him away, tell me where you have laid Him, and I will take Him away." Consumed with sorrow and blinded with grief, she was unable to see Jesus—even though He stood before her.

Think of the times when the circumstances of your life blind you from recognizing His blessed presence. He calls us by name, as He did Mary. He desires to comfort our sorrows, to give us hope, to impart a deep sense of joy and serenity that will carry us through the storms of life. But we must look through our tears and beyond them. He is with us beside every tomb. He is with us at every sick bed. He is with us in every situation, however dark. Just as Mary turned and said to Him, "Master!"—we, too, must turn our hearts toward His face, and receive the blessing He longs to give us.

My Grace is Sufficient for You   MAY 26

II Corinthians 12:2-10 and Mark 6:1-6

But He said to me, "My grace is sufficient for you, for my power is made perfect in weakness."   II COR 12:9 (RSV)

ARE WE TAKING JESUS AT HIS WORD and bringing our heavy burdens to Him? Are we accepting the grace He offers us? Not if we fret and worry about today's aches and pains. Not if we worry about what will happen tomorrow or next week.

Years ago, I knew a blessed saint of God who had spent time in a Nazi concentration camp. She had many stories to tell of the miracles God had performed for her and others during those years of untold suffering. Most of all, however, was the assurance that God was with her. That sustained her in humiliation, pain, cold, deprivations of all kinds—and the uncertainty about how long she would be allowed to live.

I try to remember that when facing some difficult times. An unexpected illness came which could not be explained nor would it go away. I searched for the root of it in my heart—and forth came some buried grief and anger I thought were long dealt with. But God showed me they were still there. As I prayed and sought the Lord, I began to accept the fact that the illness was not a waste, but that God was using it in some way beyond my understanding.

I'm sure that many of you who read these words have circumstances you find difficult. It may be pain, loneliness, or the feeling that you are forgotten by those you love. It may be bitter disappointment over the direction your life has taken. But whatever it is, it is a burden you can bring to the Lord. "My grace is sufficient for you, for my power is made perfect in weakness."

It is good to rest in the knowledge that you are greatly loved by a great God. It is good to rest in the knowledge that all your past sins and mistakes are forgiven. It is good to rest, knowing that your disappointments and griefs are all known to Him and that He will give you something better: a greater measure of His peace. Paul learned to be content with His grace. Surely we can learn that valuable lesson.

Prayer: God, of your goodness give me Yourself, for You are sufficient for me. I cannot properly ask anything less, to be worthy of You. If I were to ask less, I should always be in want. In You alone do I have all. (Dame Julian of Norwich, 1342-1443)

News! Joy! Peace! MAY 27

Titus 3:4-7 and Luke 2:8-20

But after that the kindness and love of God our Savior toward
men appeared . . ., according to His mercy, He saved us.
TITUS 3:4, 5A (KJV)

IT'S STILL NEWS, AFTER ALL THESE CENTURIES. And the world
still hasn't learned or accepted it, so we go on from one sadness to another. Yet the news and the truth are there: God has
acted to save us "according to His mercy."

When hearts open to receive the news, joy still follows. I
think of a number of souls I have known over the past thirty
years who have awakened to faith in Jesus as their personal
Lord. Without fail, I have seen new joy lighten their faces and
brighten their lives. It did not mean that all their problems disappeared or that there was no pain. What it meant was that a
new meaning had entered their lives, a new relationship with
their Creator, and a new inner harmony had begun to reveal
itself. When we open our hearts to God's "Christmas gift" to
us—the gift of His Son—joy still follows.

And what can we say about peace—that elusive and longed-
for gift? Can you remember the sense of peace and security you
felt when you were very young and your father or mother or
grandparent or some other loved one put his or her arms around
you? We all want to have a sense that we are loved and cared for,
no matter what. And that is exactly what God says to us. "The
love and kindness of God our Savior toward [us] appeared." You
are beloved of your heavenly Father. You are an object of His
love and care. That realization will bring peace when we let it
penetrate the depths of our hearts.

No Spirit of Timidity! MAY 28

II Timothy 1:1-14 and Luke 7:5-10

For God did not give us a spirit of timidity but a spirit of power and love and self-control. II TIM. 1:7 (RSV)

THE DISCIPLES PRAYED, "Lord, increase our faith!" And Jesus responded by saying if their faith was as great as a grain of mustard seed, they could move a tree into the sea. That was a dramatic way of reminding them of how small their faith really was.

What about us? Someone said recently that when things are going well, she can deceive herself about how much faith she has. But when something happens that is full of danger and threat, she realizes how little faith she has.

The same is true for me. Most of the time I *think* I believe and trust in Jesus Christ. He is my Lord and Savior. My only salvation is through His shed blood on the cross. I have accepted Him, and He has accepted me. Hallelujah!

Then some physical symptom appears that I am not prepared for. Is it serious, or just a passing annoyance? That happened recently, and finally I called our family doctor, who insisted in coming over at once. He found nothing to be alarmed about, but my blood pressure had gone up, obviously registering more fear than I wanted to admit to myself or to others! So I'm praying, "Lord, increase my faith!" I know that if there is not an ongoing trust relationship with Jesus, any unexpected threat will bring up great fear in me.

Paul was addressing this same problem when he wrote to young Timothy. He urged Timothy to "rekindle" the gift that had been given him. God has not given us a spirit of timidity, yet in spite of all He has given, some of us still retain that kind of spirit. We may even feel that we're victims of it and that it is never going to change.

I don't believe that. Our "trust relationship" with the Lord can grow, as we acknowledge and confess our fears. I have found that when I stop denying I'm afraid and start talking and praying about my fear, that the fear subsides and faith comes. Hiding our fear nourishes it. Confessing it openly—to ourselves, to the Lord, and to others—can "rekindle" the spirit God has freely given us: the "spirit of power and love and self-control."

Keeping a Good Oil Supply   MAY 29

I Thessalonians 4:13-18 and Matthew 25:1-13

But the wise took flasks of oil with their lamps.
MATTHEW 25:4 (RSV)

DID YOU EVER HAVE THE EXPERIENCE OF RUNNING OUT OF gas? This is not exactly the image we have here in Jesus' parable of the wise and foolish virgins, but it has the same meaning. The idea is that being prepared and staying prepared are very important.

Since most of us who read these pages are in what would be called "older" category (or "senior citizens"), we are often facing some serious situations and unwelcome conditions. A friend of mine recently learned that he has Lou Gehrig's disease, and even now is trying to come to grips with what that means for him. One of the things that is being seriously tested is his willingness to give up what had always seemed "a normal course" of life, and adjust himself to what has happened to him. His spiritual "oil supply" is now being tested.

During my years in the pastorate, I met people who faced such limitations with grace and faith. Others, I'm sorry to say, allowed their circumstances to plunge them into bitterness and resentment. And every one of us has the choice to make.

A good friend, now deceased, used to talk about "prepraying." Her point was that we need to prepare ourselves for the unexpected by a good, well-oiled [pun intended] relationship with the Lord. The distance between our need and Him should be very short. Daily we need to avail ourselves of what only He can give: adequate strength for anything that we have to face. He never fails those who really lean on Him.

The wise virgins went prepared for unexpected delays. We, too, need that steady willingness to pray, to believe, and to accept that in the right time and the right way, the Bridegroom will come and He will expect us to be ready.

Words to the Fearful Heart MAY 30

Isaiah 35:1-10 and Matthew 11:2-11

Say to those who are of a fearful heart, "Be strong, fear not! Behold, your God will come . . . He will come and save you."
ISAIAH 35:4 (RSV)

WHO HAS NOT KNOWN FEAR? Fear that clutches the throat, wakening us in the night hours and refusing to go away?

You may think, "What use are words like this Scripture when I am afraid? My fear is still there, and there is nothing I can do about it."

Let me share my experience. Facing coronary by-pass surgery, I knew I had a splendid surgeon and an excellent hospital. But as the time approached for the surgery, my wife would notice small signs of fear. She would say to me, "You've become afraid again. You must confess your fear to the Lord."

I wanted to be strong, so I would assure her, "No, everything's fine." But she would not give up, for she could tell what lay underneath the brave exterior. Finally I would agree to pray, "Lord, I confess that I am afraid again. I am sorry. You have never let me down. I have every reason to have faith in You. I have become afraid because I am losing control of my own life. So I ask You to forgive me, and I turn myself over to You again. I choose to put my trust in You and not in myself. And I thank

You that I can rest in You. In Jesus' name. Amen." Right away, my fear would lift.

Acknowledging our fear is one of the most important steps in dealing with it. We must remember that fear is lack of trust in God. It means we are putting our faith in ourselves.

As God leads us along the path of life, He cheers us with words of hope and promise, reminding us of His past faithfulness and training us to give up trying to control our lives, so that He might have charge. He is still teaching us that His ways are often different from the way we expect.

If you are afraid, saturate your mind with the promise and challenge of today's Scripture. A glorious and wonderful plan of God's heart is still unfolding. And remember, dear friend, that His glorious plan includes *you.*

Look Up and Lift Up Your Heads   MAY 31

Psalm 25:1-10 and Luke 21: 25-36

When these things begin to come to pass, then look up, and lift up your heads, for your redemption draweth nigh.
LUKE 21:28 (KJV)

I AM BASICALLY A FEARFUL PERSON, and it does not take very much to bring that reality up in me. So when I read today's Scripture, it seemed to be speaking again to our fear.

Much of our fear, I believe, is rooted in guilt. What does it mean? That we have failed to live up to God's standards—and not our own. We may rationalize all we like, but our conscience accuses us, and in the presence of some illness or unwanted threat to our lives, we become fearful. We wonder if hard things have happened because of our failures.

And that is where the Gospel shines in its most beautiful and brilliant light. For if we know we are afraid, and admit it to ourselves and to God, then we begin to look at the root of our fear—and our guilt and our lack of trust in our heavenly Father. And when we confess that "He is faithful and just and will forgive us our sin." (I John 1:9) I have found this to be a most helpful process in coping with fear.

Looking at the future can be a fearful thing. We do know that we will not live earthly lives forever, so we must be prepared to lay them down. Jesus showed us how: by trusting His Father when He endured the Cross. His last word was: "Father, into Thy hands I commend my spirit." That is what we are supposed to be preparing ourselves to do. By committing our way to Him day by day, we will be able to lift up our heads and know that our redemption draws nearer every step of the way.

Jesus tells us to "look up and lift up your heads." I take that to mean that we are supposed to look at the future with hope, not with foreboding. Whatever the future holds, He will be faithful and He will not desert us.

Pilgrims Together

For *where two or three*
come together in my name,
there am I with them.

MATTHEW 18:20 (NIV)

Living with an Unknown Illness

At the age of 73, I am going into my sixth year as the host of some ailment which has defied the medical experts. Lupus-like symptoms multiplied and took half my lung capacity; severe arthritic pains make me act "twice" my age, and so on. But the ailment remains unnamed and erratic.

Couple this with the left-over results of a moderate coronary twenty-two years ago, recurring angina after a triple by-pass of fifteen years ago, and it is not too hard to imagine that I have moments of darkness and anxiety.

How am I living with this condition? I wish I could say, "In the victory of faith!" but that is not always the case. Sometimes, in the night watches, I awake in pain and have to fight the feeling of being abandoned and alone. Fear and panic are very near the surface, and the battle is joined. The big problem seems to be in my mind, when it is easy to forget how many times God has delivered me, and how gracious He has been through it all. I allow myself to revert back to a childlike fear of the dark and of being alone.

I have found, however, that this is a *spiritual* battle. The psalmist says, "You shall not fear the terror of the night." There are weapons to fight the thoughts and feelings, and when I remember to use them, peace comes—sometimes slowly, sometimes quickly. These weapons are *thanksgiving and praise.* We may not think of them as weapons, but they are, and they drive away the lies that are suggested to our minds, that God is not present, that He is not able to help, or that He doesn't care. Remembering, thanking, and praising Him for past mercies are better antidotes than fear-filled petitions!

Am I learning to use faith I have to move me forward and to drive away fear? Yes, but not yet enough. I have to take it a day at a time, and refuse to let my imagination project future possibilities. Whatever is "out there" in the future, God will be there, too. That is enough, and when I choose to believe that, peace comes.

Hal M. Helms.

When Tears are Dry   JUNE 1

Revelation 21:1-6 and John 13:31-35

*God Himself will be with them; He will wipe away every tear
from their eyes, and death shall be no more, neither shall there
be mourning nor crying nor pain any more, for the former things
have passed away.*   REV. 21:3B, 4 (RSV)

D O YOU REMEMBER HAVING YOUR MOTHER OR FATHER wipe
the tears from your eyes when you had come to them with
some pain or problem? There is something infinitely comforting about that picture.

Our Heavenly Father understands our hurts and pains and
is involved in them Himself. Our pains are not permanent. Our
problems are not everlasting. They are passing phenomena, and
this image of our Heavenly Father bending over us to comfort
us is very reassuring.

I am reminded of a little verse by St. Teresa, translated by
Longfellow:

> Let nothing disturb thee,
> Nothing affright thee;
> All things are passing;
> God never changeth;
> Patient endurance
> Attaineth to all things;
> Who God possesseth
> In nothing is wanting;
> Alone God sufficeth.

Self-pity and depression are always near at hand if we allow
the hurts and disappointments of life to rule over us. But we can
either keep them "in perspective" or we can let them grow into
monstrous proportions. We are pilgrims and strangers here on
earth, and our true home is in heaven—with God. In that
blessed place, "death shall be no more, neither sorrow nor crying nor any more pain." These things will have done their work

in us, preparing us for something we can now only dimly grasp by faith. But if we keep that hope alive, we can walk through the shadows of the present, knowing that the sun is still shining, God is still God, and we are being safely led to our home with Him.

A Sacred Mystery   JUNE 2

Philippians 2:5-11 and Luke 10:29-40

And being found in human form He humbled Himself and
became obedient unto death, even death on a cross.
PHILIPPIANS 2:8 (RSV)

Through His prophet, God said:
    For my thoughts are not your thoughts,
        neither are your ways, my ways, says the Lord.
    For as the heavens are higher than the earth,
        so are my ways higher than your ways
        and my thoughts than your thoughts.
(Isaiah 55:8, 9 RSV)

WHO CAN COMPREHEND GOD'S WAYS? For the sake of His glory, His Son is humbled; for the sake of victory, He is defeated; for the sake of joy, He bears our sorrows; for the sake of life, He dies. The maker of all things submits Himself to His creation. The source of all power subjects Himself to man's weakness and cowardice.

All of our sin and sorrows, the destiny of all human history, the holy and complete purposes of God, rode upon the shoulders of Jesus.

Jesus' Palm Sunday ride leads to the walk up Golgotha. It is a joyful day, because we know that our Salvation is at hand. But it is equally woeful, because of the price He would pay for its delivery.

Nevertheless, it was a ride of triumph, a victory march,

which compelled the crowds to cheer. Jesus welcomed the shouts of praise, all the while knowing they would soon be howls of scorn. "Hosanna!" would turn to "Crucify!" And yet both are victory cries in God's eyes.

" . . . at the name of Jesus
    every knee shall bow,
in heaven and on earth,
    and under the earth,
and every tongue confess that
    Jesus Christ is Lord,
to the glory of God the Father." (Philippians 2:10-11 NIV)
Amen.

The Set of the Mind

JUNE 3

Ezekiel 37:1-14 and Romans 8:6-11

To set the mind on the flesh is death, but to set the mind on the Spirit is life and peace. ROMANS 8:6 (RSV)

To PAUL, THE WORD "FLESH" SUMS UP THE ENTIRE ASPECT OF our life which is separated from God and from God's purposes. It does not refer simply to the physical body and its various appetites. He also means it to include pride, selfishness, self-righteousness, bitterness, hard heartedness, to name a few. If we understand how broad a meaning it has, we can better think about the fleshly mind-set.

Ezekiel saw a valley filled with dry bones. They had no life. Everything that would impart life was missing. Those bones are a picture of what can happen and what does happen to us, if we allow our minds to be "set on the flesh." And then, in obedience to the Lord, Ezekiel spoke, "prophesied" to the bones, and life came. When God's Spirit came upon their dry, dead, condition, life sprang into being. What a wonderful truth! When we feel dry and dead, lifeless, hopeless, "down-in-the-mouth," we can change the set of our minds and experience one of God's greatest miacles. Without any outward change, everything changes!

Bitterness and jealousy can be washed away and we can find the gracious forgiveness and cleansing of Jesus Christ for all our sins and failures. New peace, new joy and new life springs up. All this, without any change in other people or the circumstances of our life.

In the word of Ella Wheeler Wilcox "'Tis the set of a soul that decides its goal, and not the calm or the strife."

Abiding   JUNE 4

1 John 3:18-24 and John 15:1-9

If you abide in me, and my words abide in you, ask whatever you will and it shall be done for you. As the Father has loved me, so have I loved you; abide in my love.   JOHN 15:7, 9 (RSV)

WOULD IT NOT BE FAIR TO SAY THAT WE are a striving people rather than an abiding people? Jesus is saying something very important here but most of us have never really let ourselves believe the full truth of it. Being in Christ is not a matter of achievement. In the Epistle reading, John says very plainly, "This is His commandment, that we should *believe* in the name of His son Jesus Christ and *love* one another." Of course we show what we love and what we believe by the way we act, and John makes that very clear. But love is still an inward thing, and believing is a matter of the heart—and *these,* he says are the commandments which we please God by keeping.

Jesus used the picture of a grapevine to illustrate what He was telling us. All it does is to receive nourishment from the soil, the rain and the sun and then respond according to what it is inside. It is an internal process we cannot see. The Lord says that our life in Him is like that—something internal, in the heart, hidden from the eyes of all. The only thing that reveals our fruit is the way we respond to our life situation in particular. If His life is hidden in our hearts, we can meet all circumstances, good or bad, with new courage, faith and hope.

Stay. Be fixed. Stand pat. Sit tight. Or sit loose, if you prefer. One dear old lady who was asked the secret of her long, peaceful life answered, "I sit loose, and when I worry, I sleep!" Not a bad formula. Don't fret away the hours, yearning for things that cannot be, resentful for things that are. Abide in the true Vine, whose life is given for you and whose life is in you as you open yourself to Him in faith. Let Him be your joy, your hope and your rest.

Found   JUNE 5

I Timothy 1:12-17 and Luke 15:1-10

Rejoice with me, for I have found my sheep which was lost.
LUKE 15:6B (RSV)

The saying is sure and worthy of full acceptance, that Christ Jesus came into the world to save sinners. And I am the foremost of sinners.   I TIMOTHY 1:15 (RSV)

OUR CAT LEFT THE HOUSE TWO DAYS AGO, and did not return overnight. Another day passed, and he was still gone. We began to get worried. Then just this morning, he sat outside the door, waiting to come in. He was muddy, disheveled-looking, but not harmed. You couldn't exactly say we found him, but we were very thankful when he was no longer lost to us.

Jesus says there is great joy in heaven when one sinner turns to God. I know there is joy on earth when someone dear to us "comes to himself" and begins to pray. We know that something inside, something very important is happening. Somehow we know that a soul is being changed and prepared for a better life.

Paul never got over the wonder at having been found. He

was so determined to be right, and to keep the faith—only to discover he had been missing the point of it all. After he saw the vision of Jesus on the Damascus Road, he knew that he had been lost, but now was found; and in this letter to Timothy just after describing his experience, he bursts into praise: "To the King of ages, immortal, invisible, the only God, be honor and glory for ever and ever. Amen!"

That is probably what made Isaac Watts' hymn such a favorite of John Wesley's. "I'll praise my Maker while I've breath!" Years ago I heard a teacher say that John Wesley, when he was dying, raised his head from the pillow and said, "I'll praise!" Then he fell back on the pillow. He tried it two more times, but was too weak to get out the whole line of this hymn. And she added, "What a way to die, with a triple 'Praise' on his lips."

We are a "found" people. It is not we who find, but the Shepherd who has found us. He has reached our hearts with His love, and bid us to learn day by day to love, obey, and trust Him. Yes, we once were lost but now are found. What joy!

Because He Lives   JUNE 6

Isaiah 25:6-9 and Luke 24:1-12

But the angel said to the women, "Do not be afraid: for I know that you seek Jesus who was crucified. He is not here, for He has risen, as He said."   MATTHEW 28:5, 6A (RSV)

EASTER HAS A LOT TO SAY ABOUT DEATH. We come to the Easter story in the four Gospels after having been given detailed accounts of Jesus' passion—the suffering , pain, humiliation, and injustice He experienced. And in each of those Gospels He had warned His disciples ahead of time of what awaited Him, but He had assured them that death would not be the end.

On that first Easter those faithful women who had followed Jesus and served Him and His disciples hastened to the tomb where He had been hastily laid on Friday. The women hoped, in spite of the watch and seal, that they could find a way to complete His unfinished burial preparations. Once they arrived at the tomb, they saw the stone was rolled away and the tomb was empty. Then Mary and some of the others reported that they had actually seen Jesus *alive*. It was too good to be true, but it was true! It *is* true!

All of this was to give us the assurance that we are destined for something so far beyond our imagination that we cannot conceive it. We can live *knowing* that death does not have the last word! Jesus' resurrection gave the disciples new courage and sent them out to face danger and hardship with this new knowledge that He was alive.

In our life, we, too, have to face suffering and hardship. A couple struggled through the brief life of a little child and then faced its loss. At the funeral they chose the hymn, "Because He lives, I can face tomorrow." That sentiment is the absolute bedrock on which to build our lives. This still seems too good to be true. But it *is* true, and we can live in the brightness, the joy and the wonder of it.

So That You May Know JUNE 7

John 17:6-19 and I John 5:1-13

I write these things to you who believe in the name of the Son of God, so that you may know that you have eternal life.
I JOHN 5:13 (RSV)

THE AGED APOSTLE JOHN WROTE THESE SHORT LETTERS to his Christian friends who were part of a new and very small movement. There were scattered bands of believers who often had to hide from the authorities to keep from being jailed—or worse. The apostle was concerned for them, and he wanted to give them encouragement. So, under the inspiration of the Holy

Spirit, he wrote these little letters, telling them some of the important truths he wanted them to hold onto. Almost at the end of this First Letter, he says, "I write these things to you who believe in the name of the Son of God, so that you may *know* that you have eternal life."

Most of the time we don't worry about whether we have eternal life or not. We believe, and we go struggling on with daily cares and concerns. Sometimes we feel very strong in faith, and sometimes doubts creep in. But there come times when we need to know that we have been given a summons to eternity. He did not create us just to pass out of existence like a burning comet hurtling through the sky. He created us to live with Him and to have a relationship with Him. John calls that relationship "eternal life." It is more than length. It is a life that is related to the God of all mercy and grace through Jesus Christ. Doubts will come. But beyond the clouds and darkness there is this clear word. It is given to us that we may "know" that we have eternal life in Him. What a gift!

Wonderful Words of Life   JUNE 8

I Thessalonians 3:9-13 and Luke 21:25-33

*Heaven and earth will pass away, but my words
will not pass away.*   LUKE 21:33 (RSV)

AN ENGLISH CLERGYMAN DURING THE LAST CENTURY was moving from his church to locate in another parish. He was sad about leaving his people and the place he had come to love. Late that afternoon as he looked across to the lovely old stone church, these lines began to come:

*Abide with me; fast falls the eventide,
The darkness deepens; Lord with me abide.
When other helpers fail and comforts flee,
Help of the helpless, O abide with me.*

Swift to its close ebbs out life's little day,
Earth's joys grow dim, its glories pass away;
Change and decay in all around I see,
O, Thou who changest not, abide with me.

I do not know whether the story is true, but I know that the thoughts of those lines have touched many hearts since they were first penned. I suppose, too, that as one grows older, the truth of them becomes more apparent.

Against what the prayer book calls "the changes and chances of this mortal life," stand these immortal words of our Lord Jesus Christ: "Heaven and earth shall pass away."

Stop. Wait. What is He saying? Change and decay. This world is not eternal. It will pass away. Period. It is not meant to be eternal, and one day it will be replaced, as the Bible promises, with a "new heaven and a new earth." What that means we do not know, but the process of change and decay we know very well!

"My words will not pass away." Aha! Think of that. There is something that is permanent. There is something that will last forever. There is something we can rely on, put our faith in, hang our hope on. And what is that? The words which Jesus spoke. The truth from His heart and mouth. What He tells us about life, about death, about God, about ourselves. These are words of life—worth thinking on, meditating on, "inwardly digesting."

At one point in Jesus' ministry, people were turning away, offended by what He said. He asked His disciples, "Will you go away also?" Peter answered: "Lord, to whom shall we go? You have the words of eternal life." In the midst of a world that is passing away we can hear and believe these wonderful words of life!

Made Perfect in Weakness   JUNE 9

Psalm 48 and II Corinthians 12:2-10

My grace is sufficient for you, for power is made perfect in weakness. II COR. 12:9 (RSV)

Is ANYTHING MORE UNWELCOME THAN THE FEELING of weakness or helplessness? I think of the TV ad we see, showing elderly people trying to open a container of pain relievers. The desire to be strong and capable is all but universal among human beings.

Paul knew that feeling, because something in his life prevented him from having the strength and health he desired. Believing in God's healing power and prayer, he went before the Lord with his case. "Three times I pleaded with the Lord to take it away from me. But He said to me, 'My grace is sufficient for you, for my power is made perfect in weakness.' (II Cor. 12:8, 9A NIV)

How is God's power made perfect in our weakness? Paul's answer to that was that it was for his own good that God had allowed the weak condition to remain.

I think of two friends who have undergone the most severe kind of physical illness. One of them has been given the best news possible after months of intense suffering and uncertainty. The inward change in this person, however, has been even more remarkable. His relationship with God has undergone a marked transformation. God's power has been made perfect in the weakness of His child.

My other friend is facing a terminal illness. We who know him have been amazed at the change within him as he faced increasing physical limitations. God has not abandoned him, even though healing does not seem at this point to be forthcoming. The inner change, which is always more important than physical change, has been taking place.

What does this tell us about our own situations—frustrating and sometimes discouraging? Does it not remind us that

God's view is the long view? His immeasurable love stretches way ahead of our three or fourscore years. He is preparing every one of us for an eternity far beyond anthing we have known on this earth. As Paul sums it up: "I consider that our present sufferings are not worth comparing with the glory that will be revealed in us." Romans 8:18 (NIV)

No Fear In Love   JUNE 10

I John 4:7-21 and John 15:1-8

He who fears is not perfected in love   I JOHN 4:18B (RSV)

A VERY GOOD FRIEND OF MINE IS NOW UNDERGOING A painful, dangerous, and very sophisticated procedure intended to save his life. Without it the only prognosis was of an early and painful death, so the doctors decided to proceed. For many months we talked of the whole process of his illness and what he could do about it. Now he is having to put into practice the lessons God has taught him and actively call to mind the many ways in which God has already aided him. To me that is a picture of what so many of us have to go through. God proves His faithfulness over and over to us. Yet with each new step or each new crisis, we face the same choice: will we trust or will we fear?

John must have known that when he wrote those words to the early Christians. They were certainly in "fearful" situations, with their very lives in danger. He says bluntly, "He who fears is not perfected in love." In other words, there is something "unloving" about our fear. Think about it: fear separates us from a sense of God's goodness and presence. We are inwardly *alienated* from the very One who can overcome our fear. We must unmask its true nature: that is lack of love on *our* part, perhaps lack of gratitude for all God has already done for us, or a demand that we be spared from all unpleasantness. These open us up to this unwelcome visitor *fear*, which can make us cross, grumpy, and difficult for others to be with, too!

"He [or she] who fears is not perfected in love." God is in the ongoing business of perfecting us in love and our cooperation will speed the process along. We can acknowledge with sorrow that we accuse Him through our fear, and affirm over and over that we know He does all things well. Fear cannot live long in that atmosphere!

Children of God   JUNE 11

Romans 8:9-17 and Matthew 13:1-9; 18-23

When we cry, "Abba! Father!" it is the Spirit Himself bearing witness with our spirit that we are the children of God.
ROMANS 8:15B, 16 (RSV)

AS WE GET OLDER, WE HAVE AN OPPORTUNITY to reorder our priorities. It is a God-given time to think again about what is most valuable and most important in our lives.

I would suggest that today's text offers us all a clue in this matter. We have lived through enough of life's ups and downs, its cares and its rewards to know that there is always some sense of disappointment even in the best of times, and always grace to bear even the worst of them. What can sweeten pain and sorrow? Is anything more powerful than to have the knowledge that God *is* and that we are His beloved children? I think that is perhaps *the* most important thing we ever learn. When Karl Barth was asked what was the most important thing he had learned, he answered without hesitation, "Jesus loves me, this I know, for the Bible tells me so."

After all is said and done, life's greatest realities can be reduced to pretty simple things: love of family, respect for oneself, the willingness to put others before ourselves, and the knowledge that we are God's beloved children. When the reality of that begins to "penetrate" the deep recesses of our minds and hearts, it brings peace, joy, and hope. We do not face a tragedy at the end of this earthly life, when our strength is spent and our work is done. We face a home-going, a glad return to our Father's house. All of life is meant to be a journey toward that end.

Yes, the Spirit bears witness with our spirit that we are children of God. And when He overcomes our disbelief, when He finds His way into our aloneness, we know that we are not alone. That is what Jesus brought to us, and that is worth more than all the silver and gold in the world.

Angels Unawares JUNE 12

Genesis 18:1-4, Hebrews 13:1-8, and Luke 14:1, 7-14

Do not neglect to show hospitality to strangers for thereby some have entertained angels unawares. HEBREWS 13:2 (RSV)

LET'S TALK ABOUT HOW WE CAN SERVE GOD and others right where we are. No matter what our circumstance, there are many ways every day that we can "show hospitality" to others. For what is hospitality but the welcoming of another person into our hearts and lives.

Recently I was invited to be interviewed on a local cable TV program about authors and books. The interviewer was a woman who had made a new life for herself since her husband died some years ago. I had not met her before and was a bit apprehensive about the whole experience. Within minutes, however, I was made to feel that I was among friendly people. The graciousness and hospitality of my interviewer made the entire time enjoyable. She had simply done what she had trained herself to do over the years—made me feel at home with her.

We don't have a choice about who will come into our lives or whether they will be cheerful or grumpy, eager to serve our needs or to let us serve theirs. But we do have a choice as to what we shall do with those whom we meet today. We can regard them as divinely given opportunities to show God's love or we can simply take them for granted. We can seek to be channels of grace, graciousness, hospitality, friendliness and cheerfulness, even if some of them make such effort difficult indeed! And in so doing, we will become better persons, larger-hearted persons, more able to meet tomorrow's guests with a loving expectancy.

We do not know what hidden blessings are to be brought to us today, if we keep in mind that our calling, our responsibility, our privilege, is to "show hospitality," to make others welcome and glad to be part of our lives.

The Unseen Presence JUNE 13

Romans 13:1-10 and Matthew 18:21-35

For where two or three are gathered in my name,
there am I in the midst of them. MATTHEW 18:20 (RSV)

YEARS AGO, WHEN PEOPLE USED TO CHOOSE HYMNS during the Sunday evening service, a frequent choice was "In the Garden." People like this hymn because it speaks of being alone with Jesus as a time of deep spiritual awareness and closeness.

Today's text turns our eyes away from those blessed times when we are alone with Jesus and reminds us of our need to find Him in company with others. God did not intend that our spiritual walk should be a lonely one. As Christians we are called into a goodly and holy fellowship, His Church.

We would be mistaken, however, to think of the "two or three" as being simply gathered in a service of some kind. There are many occasions when what Jesus is saying applies. It might be right in the home, where two or three family members are sharing time together. It might be when you and a friend talk about the most ordinary things, when your heart is warmed to love, to care, to send up a silent prayer to God for his or her need. Jesus says that when these humble meetings take place, "There am I in the midst of them."

The two or three might be when your pastor or a church member calls and takes you by the hand, and you know that another Person is present, adding His blessing to your conversation and prayer. Even when you are reading these words, that same promise applies. And when you read your Bible, you are in company with the apostles and martyrs—the goodly fellowship of faithful people in all ages.

In Psalm 149 we read that "the Lord takes pleasure in His people." Jesus takes pleasure in meeting with you and those whose life you share. He calls us to allow others to share in our lives, because through them we are able to catch new glimpses of Him and a better understanding of ourselves than we could learn on our own. We receive more of what Christ has for us through others than we can receive by ourselves. *Where two or three are gathered in my name, there am I in the midst of them.* It is His promise and His provision. Let us receive it joyfully.

We Pray for You   JUNE 14

Psalm 46 and Colossians 1:11-20

*And so, from the day we heard of it [your faith] we have not
ceased to pray for you, asking that you may be filled with
the knowledge of His will. . . .*   COLOSSIANS 1:9 (RSV)

PAUL DID NOT KNOW THE COLOSSIANS PERSONALLY. They were not among those to whom he had been privileged to carry the Gospel in person. "We have heard of your faith," he says earlier in this first chapter, "and the love you have for all the saints." Although he did not know them personally, he felt bound by the same love and same faith that made their hearts one. Paul had not ceased to pray for the Colossian Christians.

And prayer is a great opportunity for us to expand our concerns to include one another.

A best-selling book says, "Life is difficult." That may sound trite, but it is almost profound, because it is a truth many of us want to avoid. Life *is* difficult, and there are no lives that are not difficult, however smooth and easy they may look on the outside. Everyone has fear, worries, pains, and disappointments. So we need each other. We need the support of one another's love, care, and prayers. And the wonderful thing about prayer is that it is not geographically bound. Paul could pray for the Colossians although he had never been to their city. And we can pray for one another, even though we may never meet in this world. No matter what the circumstances, we can always pray. We can pray not only for those near and dear to us, but for anyone we know having a difficult time. And so I pray for you who read this message: that God will reveal His love and mercy to you in a special way.

Three Admonitions JUNE 15

Psalm 145:1-14 and Hebrews 10:11-14, 19-25

Let us draw near with a true heart. . . Let us hold fast the
profession of our faith . . . Let us consider one another . . .
HEBREWS 10:22-24 (KJV)

IN THE LETTER OF JAMES WE ARE TOLD, "Draw near to God, and He will draw near to you." (James 4:8) Our human life is stunted and dwarfed unless we are rightly related to our Creator and Father, who is the Source of real life.

Have you noticed that we don't always draw near to Him when things are going well? We are by nature "independent creatures," and it is always something of an effort to turn to God when things are going the way we like them. Then when things go the way we don't like them, we can either try to struggle through by our own strength, or, if we are wise, we can wake up to the fact that if we draw near to Him, He will draw near to us.

Trouble, however, brings out not only the opportunity to learn to know God better, but also to experience His goodness and mercy in new ways. But trouble can also brings the temptation to withdraw into ourselves, become bitter and hard and shut out what little sunshine there may be left in life.

Recently I saw a TV program of a festival in a small English town where people were singing old spirituals and Gospel hymns. One of the songs they sang expressed an important thought: "I shall not be moved!" "Let us hold fast the profession of our faith without wavering," especially when it really counts. When we are tempted to doubt God's goodness.

The final word our writer gives us is: "Let us consider one another to provoke to love. . ." He is saying that no matter what our trouble may be, there are others we can help. Look around and see who might need that encouraging word. We do not live alone; we do not die alone. Let us learn to be considerate of others as we go—and we will find an extra blessing waiting for us.

What is Important to You? JUNE 16

James 3:16-4:6 and Mark 9:30-37

For on the way they [the disciples] had discussed with one another who was the greatest . . . And He [Jesus] took a child and put him in the midst of them; and taking him in His arms, He said to them, "Whoever receives one such child in my name receives me." MARK 9:34, 36-37A (RSV)

DOES IT NOT ENCOURAGE YOU TO SEE HOW JESUS dealt with His disciples? He never ceased trying to teach them what was truly important and what was worthless. Over and over again through the Gospels, we see Him pointing out the difference between what is lasting and what is temporal, what pleases God and what brings suffering into our lives.

Yet we seem to have a hard time learning and living them! The old Adam in our nature seeks to put *self* first. And we do it in a thousand ways. Here are some that come to my mind. Perhaps you can think of others out of your own experience.

1. We insist on having our own way whenever possible. We may even get angry when we have to give in to someone else's way instead of our own.

2. We feel sorry for ourselves when others neglect us. Instead of being surprised and glad when they remember us, we expect that they will think of us and serve our needs.

3. We get jealous of others who seem to have it better or easier than we do. Or who seem to be "getting away with it."

4. We think ten times more about our own needs than the needs of others around us. And even if we do think of others' needs, do we not expect to be thanked and loved in return?

Jesus didn't scold the disciples when they argued about who would be first or greatest. He showed them a little child. The child symbolizes one who cannot care for himself. A child needs attention, parents, food, and shelter. He doesn't need to be "great" or "important." He needs love. And Jesus says if we give love to such a person, we actually give love to Him and to our Heavenly Father.

Life is short and sometimes difficult. It is easy to get centered on ourselves. But if we will look around at others who also are in need, even if we can only pray for them or do some small act of caring, we will be blessed. What is important to you? I think we all know what is important in the mind and heart of our Lord.

Ambassador in Chains JUNE 17

Psalm 84 and Ephesians 6:10-20

. . ."Pray also for me that I will fearlessly make known the mystery of the gospel, for which I am an ambassador in chains."
EPHESIANS 6:19, 20 (NIV)

THE PHRASE "AMBASSADOR IN CHAINS" has caught the attention of many a preacher over the centuries. Everyone knows that ambassadors are supposed to be treated in a special way. In some countries they are "above the law," and the severest punishment for them, should they break the law, would be to expel them back to their own land.

Paul had come to see his role in life as an ambassador of Jesus Christ, an appointed representative of the Savior of mankind. In II Corinthians 5:20, he writes, "We are therefore Christ's ambassadors, as though God were making His appeal through us. We implore you on Christ's behalf: Be reconciled to God." That was his message from on high, pure and simple. A plea from the heavenly Father to His lost children: be reconciled to Me. Paul found that when he preached that word, many people were offended, and as a result he ended up "in chains" in a Roman prison.

Let's shift our thoughts now to another direction. Many of us are in some sense "in chains." We are no longer able to move about with the freedom we once enjoyed, and we find our lives more circumscribed than we would like. It may be age, or illness, or some responsibility that "ties us down." Does that mean that we have to see ourselves as victims with nothing to do? God forbid! Paul was literally chained to his place, but he did not lose any opportunity to let people know that God was saying, "Be reconciled."

Most of us won't be comfortable with such a bold approach as that. But if the opportunity presents itself, we should always be ready to give an account of the faith that is in us. Because God wants his love to reach everyone we meet, we can be ambassadors by telling others how much He means to us, no matter what our circumstances.

Out of Many One   JUNE 18

I Corinthians 12:1-11 and John 2:1-11

There are many varieties of working, but it is the same God who inspires them all in every one. I COR. 12:6 (RSV)

ONE OF THE GREATEST BLESSINGS GOD HAS GIVEN US in this life is the variety of gifts. No two of us are exactly alike, and it is in this wonderful "difference" that we are shaped and molded as persons.

Most of us who are "maturing" may think that we are pretty well set in our thoughts, beliefs, and habits. Yet we are called on to relate to people who are different from us, and who see things from a different perspective. Do we not enjoy those who are still learning, still growing, still open to others—no matter what their age? It is a challenge to each of us to let the "variety of gifts" in others be a source of blessing to us.

Paul was addressing a situation in the Corinthian church in which some people were jealous of others' gifts. And it is easy to get envious or jealous of those who seem to have more talent, more freedom, more *personality* than we have. Paul is saying, whatever the gift, it is given by the one and same Spirit, for the good of all.

Recently I was taken to the emergency ward of a small hospital because of a sudden allergic reaction. Lying there in the "middle of the night," I was able to be thankful that each of the staff seemed willing to use his or her expertise to alleviate my unpleasant symptoms. My own need was an occasion of seeing how the "variety of gifts" worked for my good.

Today you will be the recipient of some of these various

gifts in others. I don't know what they will be, but I hope you will be alert to them, and find yourself giving thanks that God, in His love for you, has given you others with gifts that enlarge and bless your life. "There are varieties of working, but it is the same God who inspires them all in every one."

Saying Thank You JUNE 19

Deut 8:1-10 and James 1:17-27

And you shall bless the Lord your God for the good land He has given you. DEUT 8:10B (RSV)

Every good endowment and every perfect gift is from above, coming down from the Father of lights, with whom there is no variation or shadow due to change. JAMES 1:17 (RSV)

THANKSGIVING IS BASIC, AND ESSENTIAL TO OUR SOULS. It is not a specific day that concerns us here, but an attitude and activity of our hearts. We might say that thanksgiving is as vital to the heart as air is to the lungs. Without it, the heart shrivels, dries up, encloses on itself, and dies.

Thanksgiving can be practiced anywhere, at any time, on any occasion. "Have no anxiety about anything," says St Paul, "but in everything by prayer and supplication *with thanksgiving* let your requests be made known to God." (Phil 4:6)

How many times our grumpy dispositions and short tempers would simply disappear if we remembered to be thankful! And what a return we get, when we remember that a "thank you" from the heart gladdens others who may be carrying burdens we know nothing about.

Several years ago, I felt the urge to write to a high school teacher whose class I attended in 1938 to thank her for what she had meant to me. She was a strict disciplinarian, but she was concerned far beyond the duty of teacher. She was always willing to spend extra time with any of us who might have a problem, and continued her interest even after we had moved on to higher grades. My note had to be addressed to a Presbyterian home for the aged where she then lived at the age of ninety. After a few weeks, I received a reply, written in a shaky but familiar handwriting, saying how glad she had been to get my note. She even remembered a little gift I had once given her. So what began as a desire to gladden someone else by saying "Thank you for what you did for me" was returned to gladden my own heart.

Perhaps there are "Thank you's" that you can make this week. Now is a great time for receiving the blessing that will come when you say "Thank you" to someone else.

The thankful heart is the glad heart, and brings greater healing than many a medical prescription.

How Often Must I Forgive? JUNE 20

Romans 14:5-12 and Matthew 18:21-35

Then Peter came up and said to Him, "Lord, how often shall my brother sin against me, and I forgive him? As many as seven times?" MATT 18:21 (RSV)

I SUPPOSE THAT FORGIVING IS THE HARDEST thing we are asked to do.

Let's talk first about the imagined wrongs, the slights, and hurts we take to ourselves that may not have been intended. We are all guilty of these at times, and they can be a real problem in our relationships. They can fester and incubate for years if we do not allow God to show us the truth about them and get on with the process of forgiveness.

We repress the exact memory of what has hurt us or made us angry—but the feeling lies there, waiting to do its deadly work. It can be very helpful sometimes to start writing down some of these feelings of unfairness, slights, neglects, and so on. If we get them out of our secret storehouses, we can lay them before God and ask Him for grace to *forgive,* or for His mercy in forgiving us for carrying them in our hearts.

There is another kind of forgiveness, though, that we must look at. Sometimes we have been truly wronged. An unfaithful spouse. A brutal parent. A cruel teacher. An unreasonable boss. We experience actual hurt and there is a wound left in our souls. What can be done? Remembering will certainly not cure it. Neither will forgetting, because, if it is merely repressed, it is still alive. Jesus gives the *only* solution. It is the solution God provided on the Cross for all the hurts we have inflicted upon Him. Forgiveness. Actually letting go of the demand that "justice" be done. "Father, forgive them . . ."

Forgiveness in this case is going to affect us more than it does the person who has offended. It will begin to remove the gall and bitterness of soul that can corrode and destroy. Is there a situation or a person in your life that you have not yet forgiven?

Being Reconciled   JUNE 21

II Corinthians 5:16-21 and Luke 15:11-32

We beseech you on behalf of Christ, be reconciled to God.
II COR 5:20B (RSV)

HERE IS A STRANGE WORD, when you really think about it. It is God's appeal to us to be reconciled to him.

Have you ever had an important relationship that suffered a break, a serious rupture? And if so, do you remember how important it was to have it reconciled? Or perhaps you were aggrieved, and would not allow reconciliation to take place. In either case, suffering was involved.

Two places in the world are objects of prayer for this writer: northern Ireland where Christians have been "at war" with each other for centuries. A situation that harks back to the seventeenth-century has been allowed to breed ill will and enmity between people who call on the same Lord. The other place is Israel, where the relations between two ancient peoples is marked by hatred and violence. Can there be reconciliation? Only God has the answer, so it is appropriate that we send our prayers to him, for the problems are beyond human solutions. They require a heart change on both sides!

But when God sends his appeal to us, there is no need for a "heart change" on his part. He has already come to us in Jesus Christ "reconciling the world to himself." (v. 19) He does not wait for a heart change on our part to extend the hand of reconciliation.

Are there those to whom we should be reconciled in our hearts? Is there a corner of bitterness somewhere toward some one who has wronged or hurt us? If so, we can, by the help and grace of God, choose to forgive, and be reconciled in our hearts. Remember that when we hold grudges of any kind, we grieve and hinder the work of the blessed Spirit of God within us. Since God has shown us that he desires reconciliation with us, we can show the same spirit toward others.

Abide in My Love, That My Joy May Be in You

JUNE 22

Acts 2:1-21, Romans 8:14-17, and John 15:8-17

As the Father has loved me, so have I loved you; abide in my love . . .These things I have spoken to you, that my joy may be in you, and that your joy may be full. JOHN 15:9, 11 (RSV)

IF THERE IS ONE THING THAT CAN MAKE DIFFICULT circumstances bearable, it is the presence of love. For love people have suffered great pain, undergone the greatest sacrifices, done the most heroic deeds.

Love sacrifices self for others. That's what Jesus Christ did for all of us. You can hear the tenderness, the deep, mysterious caring as you read those words: "As the Father has loved me, so have I loved you." He held nothing back from his little band of friends. He loved them to the end. And these are among his final words: "Abide in my love." Don't forget it. Don't forget it. Don't get distracted and discount its reality. Remain in it by keeping His commandments. For He wants His joy, the joy He knows in pleasing God to be with you.

When the 120 gathered on that first Pentecost and the Holy Spirit came upon them, they were so filled with joy that people thought they were drunk! And such was the effect of it, that 3,000 people became believers that day, and the Church was born. Of course they we would meet disappointments, sickness, frustrations—the same kinds of things that happen to us today. But Jesus had said to them, "Remember to abide in my love." The Holy Spirit brought that truth and put it right inside their hearts—and does the same for us today. Keeping His commandments means living by His words.

His new commandment is "Love one another as I have loved you." If we put those words into practice, His love will glow in us like a warm friendly fire. Joy will come even in the midst of trials. So many have found this true that we cannot really doubt it. Put away all that denies His goodness. Let self-pity, fear, anxiety, bitterness, and anger fall away into the dust. Let His love fill your heart and shine through you today.

Weary in Well-Doing?   JUNE 23

II Thess 3:6-13 and Luke 21:5-19

Brethren, do not be weary in well-doing. II THESS 3:13 (RSV)

I SUSPECT THAT WE ALL GROW "WEARY IN WELL-DOING" at times. Paul must have known the temptation, and that is why he cautions against it in this letter to the Thessalonians as well as his letter to the Galatians. (Gal 6:9) Weariness is a matter of fatigue, and we all know how that feels.

But there is a weariness of soul, a flagging of zeal, a letting-up of our commitment to stay close to God. One of the areas in which we can grow "soul-weary" is compassion. We become cross and irritable, peevish and cantankerous if this weariness dominates us. How can we deal with it? Paul again gives the answer: "Be kind to one another, tenderhearted, forgiving one another, as God in Christ forgave you."

Another area in which we grow weary is in dealing with our own faults. It is one thing to recognize that we *have* faults we don't like. It is quite another thing to try to over-come them. Human nature is so stubborn, our patterns so ingrained, that we find ourselves slipping back into old reactions we thought we had overcome long ago. And that can be discouraging and *tiring*. Then we are tempted to give up and say, "It's just not worth the effort. People will have to accept me as I am." But that is not what we are called to as children of God. He not only saves us and loves us *as we are*, He is concerned with purging and pruning away that which keeps us from reflecting the image He created us in. We sing "I want to be like Jesus," and He takes us seriously. So when we get discouraged, "weary," remember that He urges us to carry on.

The most refreshing thing I know is to remember that the Holy Spirit makes it possible for us to achieve what we could never do ourselves. We are not left to struggle alone. He is with us and in us, so the impossible is possible—in Him.

A Cup of Water   JUNE 24

James 4:7-17 and Mark 9:38-50

*Whoever gives you a cup of water to drink because you
bear the name of Christ, will by no means lose
his reward.*   MARK 9:41B (RSV)

WHEN JESUS SAID, "IT IS MORE BLESSED TO GIVE than to receive," He was stating a truth about basic reality, not just trying to get people to give a little more to a good cause.

In today's text, He speaks of giving and receiving. He assures us that we cannot outgive God. No matter how little the gift, or how great, God will not allow us to be bigger givers than He is! You *cannot* lose your reward.

We are being told a deep spiritual truth here. If we learn to give, to turn loose whatever good thing we are offering to someone else—whether it is money, or a piece of candy, or a flower, or a kind word, or a helpful act—if we learn to give it, our reward will be greater than the gift. We will be blessed more than the receiver.

It is wonderful that Jesus uses the "cup of water" in this verse to teach his lesson. When that cup of water is given and received, you don't get it back. It's gone for good. And that's the way we should feel about anything we've given to others. Otherwise we haven't given at all. We've only deposited the good deed or the gift and are waiting for the person to pay us back.

God pays back those who give freely without demanding and don't demand anything in return. It's a spiritual principle and it always works.

> *Selfishly I waited, waiting in my need,*
> *Hoping still that someone might look and see and heed.*
> *Then I saw another, whose thirst exceeded mine,*
> *And stirred by His compassion and by His grace divine,*
> *Stretched my hand to help, though it was very hard,*
> *And found in helping someone else, an unseen, great reward.*

The Widow's Mite

Psalm 146 and Mark 12:38-44

Truly I say to you, this poor widow has put in more than all those who are contributing to the treasury. For they all contributed out of their abundance; but she . . . MARK 12:43, 44A (RSV)

IT HAS BECOME A PART OF THE COMMON LANGUAGE—"the widow's mite." That was the smallest coin that existed in that day. Jesus contrasted it with the size other people were able to give "out of their abundance." The significance of this gift was that it was everything she had.

This story reminds me of another I heard many years ago, when a church was undergoing a large building project, and people were being urged to give sacrificially. When the offering was taken up, an usher saw a widow take off her wedding ring and place it on the offering plate. The church officials felt that the only right thing was to give the ring back to the woman. To their amazement, however, she was indignant when they offered her ring back. "I did not give it to you," was her answer, "I gave it to the Lord."

That is the secret of what Jesus saw when he watched the poor woman cast in her two mites. She was giving her all to the Lord. What this story asks is this: am I really giving my all to God, or am I holding back, not trusting Him enough to give myself wholly to Him?

Jesus talked about a man given ten talents, another given five talents, and another give one talent. The point of His story was that the man who had only one talent was bitter, judged the master who entrusted it to him, and hid it in the earth, doing nothing with it. His spirit was just the opposite of that poor widow, who so loved and trusted God that she was not afraid to give all she had.

The happiest people I know are those who are not holding themselves back from giving—time, energy, prayer, concern, *and* materially if they are able. What is in our heart, prompts us either to give ourselves away or hold back, fearing to let go. The widow knew which was best!

Asking the Wrong Questions   JUNE 26

II Thessalonians 2:13 TO 3:5 and Luke 20:27-38

There came to Him some Sadducees, those who say that there is no resurrection, and they asked Him a question . . .
LUKE 20:27A (RSV)

THEY DIDN'T WANT AN ANSWER AT ALL. They had already made their minds up. They did not believe, and they wanted to make Jesus fall for a trick question.

What a surprise when He turned their question around and spoke words far beyond their understanding about the nature of the life to come! He clearly showed it to be higher, nobler, and purer than anything we have known here.

I am reminded of the times I have argued a point with others, trying to prove the rightness of my opinion, asking "incisive" questions intended to break down the other person's defenses. In such cases, there is no desire to learn, so the question is dishonest.

Then there are times when we ask the wrong question, because we know beforehand that God is not going to answer it. One person who was going through a hard time prayed, "Why me, Lord?" The answer formed very simply and clearly in her mind: "Why not you?" She was asking the wrong question, but the answer set her free from accusing God. After all, God allowed His dearly beloved Son to suffer pain and rejection. If He asks us to suffer a little, should we question His goodness?

A Catholic priest remarked some time ago, "We western Christians ask too many unanswerable questions, and we get ourselves into trouble by doing so. We need to leave many things in the realm of mystery." Think how many religious controversies have followed attempts to explain Jesus' words, "This is my Body, which is given for you." The more people try to explain it, the more they get into difficulty and controversy. I love the hymn verse that says, "I believe whate'er the Son of God hath told; What the Truth hath spoken, That for truth I hold."

So take on faith what God is giving you day by day. Do not question His goodness. Do not try to figure out all the secrets hidden in His divine plan. Know only that His will toward you is good, that He means only good for you, and that if you will trust Him, you will come to know that "He doeth all things well."

He Went About Doing Good   JUNE 27

Isaiah 42:1-9 and Acts 10: 34-38

How God anointed Jesus of Nazareth with the Holy Spirit and with power; How he went about doing good and healing all that were oppressed by the Devil, for God was with Him.

ACTS 10:38 (RSV)

WHAT A BEAUTIFUL SUMMARY OF JESUS' LIFE we have in that sentence! And what is even more wonderful is that He is still in the business of "doing good and healing all who are oppressed of the devil."

He never turned anyone in need away. Sometimes it seems His disciples were annoyed with people who came with their troubles but Jesus said, "Let them come." The picture we see of Jesus in the Gospel is of a Shepherd caring for and seeking out His sheep. And we know that the same heart beats with the eternal love of the Good Shepherd for each one of us in our need, no matter who we are.

He was able to deal with the problems that He confronted. Whether it was the problem of the demon-possessed man who continually roamed about in the graveyard, or the sick woman who touched the hem of His garment and was healed, or the widow whose son was dead and on the way to the tomb—no matter what the problem, He solved it. I think we give Him less credit than He deserves and forget that the Lord is able to take on every one of our concerns—if we are willing!

What He did then He is willing to do now. Jesus is still in the saving and healing business. His truth and His Spirit can still dispel the darkness of the devil and bring light and hope to our hearts. He is still willing to come under the burdens with which we are burdened, saying, "Come unto me and rest." So in the night time, when the hours are long; when fear grabs us by the throat and steals our peace of mind; when low-level anxiety keeps us from enjoying present blessing—we can turn to Him who "went about doing good and healing all that were oppressed of the Devil."

Looking Forward or Looking Back?   JUNE 28

Psalm 16 and Luke 9:51-62

Jesus said to him, "No one who puts his hand to the plow and looks back is fit for the kingdom of God."   LUKE 9:62 (RSV)

THIS SEEMS LIKE ONE OF JESUS' "HARD SAYINGS." He was emphasizing in the strongest terms the seriousness of our relationship with God. Half-hearted commitment meant no commitment at all.

Why was He so insistent that we allow nothing to interfere with our desire to follow Him and enter the kingdom of heaven? I believe it's because without that, we are caught in the web of hopelessness. Today we hear all kinds of things which underscore the hopelessness of life without God. Even as this is being written, the legislature of our state is debating a bill that would legalize "assisted suicide." That is just one example of where life can lead when God is left out. So Jesus is calling us to take seriously the call and the opportunity to have God in our lives.

I find, however, that "looking back" becomes a rather pleasant pastime as I grow older. I like to think of old times, old places, and relationships with people who have passed away. Is this what Jesus was condemning? I don't think so, but it is something that bears watching!

What is the Lord saying? Don't let the past enthrall you. God has a future for you. Life is not a static thing, but a journey. You cannot move forward with your face turned backward. No matter how old, how inactive we may be, God still has a purpose in our life. Let Him show you day by day that life is worth living and that the future is full of hope, if we are grounded in Him.

Ask What I Shall Do For You   JUNE 29

Matt 6:12-14, James 4:8-10, II Kings 2:1-12

When they had crossed, Elijah said to Elisha, "Ask what I shall do for you . . ." and Elisha said, "I pray you, let me inherit a double share of your spirit."   II KINGS 2:9 (RSV)

TODAY'S TEXT IS PART OF THE DESCRIPTION of the departure of the great prophet Elijah "in a chariot of fire," and the strange, bewildering events which preceded it. His protégé, Elisha, was wise enough to read the signs, to know that Elijah's earthly ministry was finished, and that his time of departure was at hand, and he wanted to be there when it happened. Elijah seems to be trying to get away from his young friend, but what he is actually doing is testing the intensity of his desire.

I see that same principle at work at times in our prayers. We ask for something we think we want, something that seems good, and do not get an immediate answer. What is going on? Is God testing us to see if we *really* mean what we are praying?

Suppose someone has hurt us, and we find a deep resentment toward that person in our hearts. And we pray something like this: "Lord, I know it's wrong not to forgive, so I pray that You will give me a forgiving spirit toward so-and-so." But we find that the resentment is still there. We still feel hurt, resentful, wronged, or neglected. Then what should we do? We should keep on praying! The problem lies in us—in our double-mindedness. Some part of us wants to punish, to get even with the person, or to have him or her "eat crow" as the saying goes.

There is a wonderful verse in Isaiah which says "You shall seek me and you shall find me, *when* you seek me with all your heart." As long as our heart is divided between wanting to forgive (like a good Christian should) and wanting to punish (like our old human nature wants to do) we should not be surprised that God does not pour out on us the spirit of forgiveness.

I am reminded of a story told by the late Corrie Ten Boom, a great Dutch Christian who was imprisoned in one of Hitler's concentration camps. Corrie's beloved father died in prison and her sister, Betsy, died a lingering, painful death in the same camp where Corrie was held, while Corrie was miraculously freed near the end of the war. However, she continued in bitterness toward those who had persecuted her family, especially one guard who had been so brutal to Betsy. Some years later, she was speaking to a large gathering, telling how God had been with her in prison and all the miracles she had witnessed. After her talk, a German approached and identified himself as that guard. He had been converted and had come to ask forgiveness for what he had done. At first, Corrie said, that bitterness rose up within her. But she knew it was wrong so she extended her hand in forgiveness. "I felt the love of God flow through me to that man," she said. She had prayed enough and sought God with all her heart—and the answer had come.

Faithful in Very Little JUNE 30

Psalm 113 and Luke 16:1-13

He who is faithful in a very little is faithful also in much; and he who is dishonest in a very little is dishonest also in much.
LUKE 16:10 (RSV)

I BELIEVE THAT MOST OF US WOULD SAY THAT OUR opportunities for service are small. Like the man in Jesus' parable of the talents, we would not classify ourselves as those with the ten talents, but identify ourselves with the poor fellow who only received one. So it might be profitable for us to think about what it means to be "faithful in very little."

My mind goes back across the years to people whom I visited while I was a pastor. In one church, there was a blind couple—both husband and wife. When I knew them they were "senior citizens," living alone, doing their own housework, and leading a "normal" life. I never heard one of them speak in bitterness or self-pity about their condition. As a way of involving themselves in the work of the Church, they knitted or crocheted squares for afghans to be sold at the annual church fair. They were great examples of people who were "faithful in a very little."

What about your opportunities for prayer? If prayer is as important as Jesus said it is, and if God has bestowed such promises on prayer, we are guilty of serious neglect if we do not pray. Moreover, it is important that we pray beyond our own small circle of concerns. If, as the poet said, "more things are wrought by prayer than this world dreams of," why do we not hold these concerns before the Lord in prayer instead of just complaining about them?

"Faithful in very little things." Think about the little things in your life. Can you be more faithful in seeking and following God's will in them? If you do, you will be both blessed and a blessing.

Appendix

Behold Your King PALM SUNDAY

Isaiah 50:4-9A and Matthew 21:1-11

*Tell the daughter of Zion, Behold, your King is
coming to you, humble and mounted on an ass.*
MATT 21:5 (RSV)

THINK OF THAT WONDERFUL SIGHT of Jesus entering
Jerusalem, the Holy City. He was the one the ancient
prophet saw only dimly, as he wrote of Him who would come
"victorious but humble." Yes, He would conquer this city, but
not in the usual way. Death itself would be defeated, by seeming weakness and defeat! God's ways often defy our human
logic and natural expectations.

The crowds recognized Him as the healer and teacher who
had caused such a stir all the way from Galilee to the region
south of Jerusalem. They nourished the hope that God would
send a leader and break their bondage, delivering them from
the cruel Roman yoke. So they hailed him according to their
expectations: "Blessed is He who comes in the name of the
Lord! Hosanna the highest!"

He disappointed them, of course. A yoke needed to be broken, but it was the yoke of sin, guilt and death. He came to set
us all free!

It is easy to be a Christian when everything is favorable.
Our real loyalty and faith are put to the test when our circumstances are hard, or we have suffered wrongs and have not forgiven those who have wronged us. We must let this time bring
us back to basics: Jesus' love for us and our love for Him.

Since it is "Holy Week" it is a good time to read the Psalms,
especially the so-called Penitential Psalms: 6, 32, 38, 51, 102,
130, and 143. Also reading a chapter each day from the
Gospels telling about Jesus' last days on earth renews our gratitude for all He is.

May you have a very blessed Holy week in which you experience the great ocean of His love.

He Goes Before You EASTER

1 Peter 1:3-9 and Mark 16:1-8

"But go, tell His disciples and Peter that He is going before you to Galilee; there you will see Him, as He told you."
MARK 16:7 (RSV)

CHRIST IS RISEN! HE IS RISEN INDEED! When a group of us visited Russia during Easter week last year, these words were heard over and over again. It was a cry of triumphant faith that had survived seventy years of brutal persecution. Only a resurrection faith could do that!

The disciples were still filled with fear when this message came. After all, their beloved leader had been seized, tortured and crucified, and they had no way of knowing how soon they might receive the same fate. They needed at least a brief time away from the danger of Jerusalem. And so this message. The main point, however, is this: Jesus went before them into all their Galilees, and He goes before us into ours. Because He was and is alive, ours is not merely a religion of memory. The Christian life is a walk with a living Presence.

Whenever we meet with a circumstance that seems too much for us, we can be sure that He has gone before us and will meet us there. All of us can remember times when life became simply too heavy to bear alone. And Jesus has never failed us. So, whatever lies ahead—that unknown future—we have His Word that He goes before us and will meet us there.

Our final and most fearful rendezvous is no different from the other times of need. Death has no power to limit His presence. Inscribed above the empty tomb we can mark the words "O grave, where is thy victory?" Christ is risen! He goes before you . . . and there He will meet you as He said. Alleluia!